RUBENS

RUBENS

PIERRE CABANNE

LONDON

THAMES AND HUDSON

TRANSLATED FROM THE FRENCH BY
OLIVER BERNARD

THIS EDITION © THAMES AND HUDSON LONDON 1967
© EDITIONS AIMERY SOMOGY S.A. PARIS 1967
PRINTED IN FRANCE

CONTENTS

Preface

Anyone who wished had access to Rubens' house; he worked there in full view of everybody, surrounded by assistants, domestic servants, collectors, admirers and even the merely curious, attracted there by his fame. Such, indeed, was the custom among the majority of the great artists of his time; whether they worked in churches, palaces or their own studios, they seldom made any attempt to evade the public gaze. But even though Rubens' work was carried out in public, his private life remains for the most part undocumented and obscure.

This favourite of not just one, but several, courts will always be surrounded by mystery, in spite of the fact that for half a century his work took him throughout the length and breadth of Europe. Right from his earliest years he learnt to live behind a mask. Personal grief, political reverses, illness—none of these ever altered the image he presented of himself to the world. His true self was something Rubens hardly ever revealed. Compared with those of Delacroix and Van Gogh, Rubens' letters, throughout his life, are conventional, uniform and cold.

When one attempts to reconstruct a past life, one cannot but risk walking on treacherous ground. In Rubens' case there is not a witness, a scrap of written evidence or even an official report, which, for whatever reason, is not to some extent suspect.

The various biographies are full of contradictions, especially where it is no longer a matter of simple facts which, in any case, are generally linked to the most important historical events of the period.

Picasso once said: 'There must surely come a time when there will be a science that one might call the science of man, the aim of which will be to see behind the creative artist the man pure and simple.'

I have tried to represent this creative artist and his work in the historical context of his time.

CHAPTER ONE

City of childhood and dreams

Spain and the Spanish Netherlands, its northern province, were ruled with a rod of iron by the Most Christian Kings who were indefatigable in pursuit of the salvation of their subjects.

The aristocracy found Philip II's dictatorship as difficult to bear as did the common people. At their head were William of Nassau, nicknamed the Silent, Prince of Orange, and Counts Egmont and Horn. On 5 April 1566 two hundred noblemen carrying mendicants' wallets and beggars' bowls to show that their cause was also that of the common people, presented themselves to Margaret of Parma, who had once been Charles V's mistress, and whom Philip, the late Emperor's son, had designated governor of the Netherlands. They submitted to her a petition bearing two thousand signatures: the famous Compromise. The Calvinists were behind this enterprise, their main aim being the suppression of the Inquisition and the restitution of civil liberties.

Margaret was moved by the sight of all these fine gentlemen dressed as beggars. She was still a very handsome woman and had had a colourful life. She listened to their complaints and even went so far as to shed a tear; their conviction was catching. 'What, Madam,' said the Comte de Berlaymont, her chief financial adviser, 'are you afraid? They are only *gueux* (beggars)!' The name stuck.

Margaret accepted the petition and allowed it to be sent to the King. The Calvinists, however, suddenly abandoned all moderation. Taking advantage of the idleness and indecision of the authorities, they broke out in revolt, destroyed or defiled the churches, dressed up in sacred vestments for sacrilegious masquerades, and sacked

1 *Philip II, c. 1630*

towns and villages under the indifferent eyes of the nobles who, though concerned by such furious behaviour, were not sorry to see this revolt against the Spanish occupation. The Regent, in a frenzy, had troops brought from Germany to reimpose law and order, while William the Silent, seeing that he could not win, refused to give his support to the Protestant army formed to resist the Spanish forces. Philip II decided to check the rebellion at once, and chose for the purpose the Duke of Alba, whose ferocity was a byword. He did not belie his reputation: the Netherlands was crushed with remorseless cruelty and on 5 June 1568 Egmont and Horn were executed. Order was restored once more throughout the land.

The Calvinists fled before the severity of the repression; the Prince of Orange went to his Nassau estates in Germany, to bide his time.

Among the refugees was Jan Rubens, a municipal magistrate of Antwerp, and his family. Being suspected of heresy he might have gone to prison or been executed, like so many others. A hundred thousand went into exile, and their defection was to be paid for by numbers of Flemish nobles and bourgeois who thought themselves safe, or trusted Philip II. In front of terrified crowds, the faggots and stakes were prepared for the burning of batches of Protestants. Hanged men swung from the trees. The 'Spanish fury' was unleashed: there was a smell of burning flesh, of clotted blood, of death.

Courtly, well-educated and refined, Jan Rubens deserves the name of humanist. He belonged to a family which had established itself in the Flemish capital in the fourteenth century; his father was an apothecary of that city; and he had, in his youth, studied at the universities of Louvain, Rome and Padua, returning from them with the spirit of enquiry and cultivated mind that made it possible for him to obtain his Doctorate *in utroque jure* and take his place, as advocate, among the most prominent citizens of Antwerp. In 1561, at the age of thirty-two, the year of his marriage, he was appointed magistrate; but a few years later it began to be rumoured that he supported the Calvinists. Disturbed by these rumours he asked to be allowed by the municipal council to testify to his standing as a good Catholic. As events began to move rapidly, however, he and his family left Antwerp for Cologne and the estates of the Prince of Orange.

The capital of Flanders had grown steadily, and the sixteenth century was the time of its greatest glory. The large port had become an enormous warehouse into which merchandise flowed from every country in the world. Along its heavily fortified quays, hardly visible to the townspeople, who could thus forget both the water and the ships from which they obtained the bulk of their wealth, the most

2 Anon, *Scene from the 'Spanish fury' in Antwerp*, 1576

diverse languages were spoken. Only New York at the beginning of the twentieth century compares in the speed of its growth with Antwerp in this period. About 1440 the town consisted of no more than 3,334 dwellings; at the end of the fifteenth century there were 6,800; and in 1550 nearly 9,000. A population of 600,000 made it necessary for the municipal authorities to extend the circle of fortifications of the town into the country, to create a new quarter of the St-Jacques parish, and to open up new highways. In 1570 the building of a new town to the north began to be planned. The trade figures of '*Antverpia, Mercatorum Emporium*' in this period reached the figure of 3,000 millions of gold francs!

Antwerp had no turbulent proletariat such as existed in many great ports; there were no assertions of social or economic rights. Peace reigned over all classes of the population, who lived in calm and prosperity. Antwerp was not only the financial capital of a large part of Europe, but also its commercial metropolis. Its influence was not limited to the vast Habsburg empire with its overseas possessions; it extended even to the territories of the Emperor's rivals, France and the Ottoman Empire; and to the nations then in the full flowering of their prosperity, Portugal and England. There was only one disturbing sign: the bankruptcy of the governments of Spain, Portugal and France in 1552. The commercial stagnation which followed had not yet been overcome when the religious troubles began.

Business had its own laws. In Antwerp itself no foreign merchant armed with a safe-conduct could be arrested; even criminals and traitors whom the whole of Europe had outlawed were safe here provided that they protected themselves with some sort of business transaction. The Church respected this state of affairs and excommunications and interdicts were suspended during fairs. Merchants and visiting brokers, like freemen of the city, paid no taxes at all, and were afforded every possible facility for carrying out their business. These freedoms and exemptions had made it possible for Antwerp to triumph over its rival Bruges. Coupled with the atmosphere of liberty which reigned in the town, they assisted the rapid and prodigious growth of the port.

3   Anon, *The Prince of Orange pacifying the Calvinists,* 1567

4 Anon, *Skating on the Scheldt in Antwerp*

Antwerp, like Amsterdam today, was crossed in every direction by
a network of canals. Its commercial zenith coincided not only with
the growth of new districts, but with the building or embellishment
of large public buildings and private dwellings, in which the traditional elements of Flemish Gothic found themselves side by side
with Italianate importations of style. The spire and tower of the
Church of Notre-Dame, built to the designs of Herman and Domien
de Waghemakers, and completed in 1521; the *Vieille Boucherie*—
now known as the Vleeshuis Museum; the frontage of the Steen;
the house of Van Liere, where Charles V and Dürer had stayed; the
old Exchange building; all these, designed by the same architects,
bear witness to such confrontations of styles, more or less harmo-

niously blended. These occur in the decoration forms of the altar-pieces which were exported from Antwerp in large quantities, as well as in the ornamentation of the façades of buildings. In the second half of the century, the Italian influence triumphs in the outward aspect of the imposingly designed town hall built from 1561 to 1564 by Cornelius de Vriendt, called Floris. The building, in spite of its structural form, which is inherited from that of the old Flemish Halls, remains the finest example of Renaissance style. Indeed the whole of Flanders experienced this encounter between the native and imported trends; but it seems that, as in painting, the Italianate represents no more than a concession to the fashion of the period. Flemish artists were inspired far more by the seductiveness and inquisitiveness of the 'modern' spirit than by Italian art as such. The Italian influence added to Flemish monuments and pictorial decorative ideas, overgrowths, complications perhaps, but hardly a style. Neither the visits of Flemish artists to Italy, nor the publication in the Low Countries of works on antique and Renaissance architecture, brought about any profound modification of the traditional Flemish outlook.

To us today, Antwerp, with its cosmopolitan character, seems to have been a kind of sixteenth-century Chicago, where adventurers, brokers and speculators were in control; where there was an atmosphere of sinister excitement, redolent of exotic spices and alcohol; where women were easily available, and knifeplay was common. The ceaseless mingling of dubious characters resulting from the wideness and scope of commercial transactions was a standing encouragement to the relaxation of moral standards. Places of prostitution had become so numerous and so prosperous that their proprietors had to be exempted from taxation. Brothels were frequented by members of the highest society, and it was even usual, as in Venice, for aristocratic ladies to be seen at the gaming tables.

The women of Antwerp were very much admired and sought-after. Even before Rubens displayed their opulent curves in his masterpieces these appetizing Flemish ladies enjoyed a European reputation. Richly bedecked with materials and jewels from the four corners of the earth, they were the queens of the city. They loved festivals and fairs, balls and entertainments, musical suppers—in fact all kinds of amusements where their beauty and love of pleasure could be given a chance to expand. Too rich, too fortunate, Antwerp went through a period of excess, unaware that the difficulties arising from the financial slump were the first signs of her imminent fall, and averting her eyes from political strife and religious crisis alike. Nor was it generally understood that the city owed its prosperity less to its own genius than to the extraordinary facilities it offered to speculators and traders of all sorts, who would have been able to operate nowhere else with such ease. Antwerp was unaware of the misfortunes which were about to overwhelm her.

Among those more perceptive people who felt anxious about the fate of the city was Jan Rubens. An irreverent and adventurous man, who liked money, gambling and women, he had far too lively a taste for liberty to remain in this happy-go-lucky city once the rumblings of revolt were heard. He would have all the time in the world, in exile, to think over what he had lost; but would he dream how great a gift he would one day make to his native country?

Money, quickly made, flowed like water. It was lavished not only upon celebrations, fine clothes and pleasure, but also upon works of art. Artists in their hundreds, hardly sufficient in number however to meet the flood of orders, were organized in the Guild of St Luke, one of the most prosperous in northern Europe. The Guild, whose origins went back to the fourteenth century, formed a kind of federal republic comprising, under the aegis of a president, four 'principal categories . . . and a score of subordinate crafts'.

Between 1491 and 1520, 358 new members joined the Guild. They included 150 painters and thirty-eight sculptors. For the 'joyous entry' into the town of the future Philip II in 1549, 233 painters and 114 sculptors assisted in the decoration of the streets. Second to artistic production in the town's activities was printing.

The creation of works of art, for the most part intended for export, played a large part in the growth of Flemish prosperity. The artists, who were known throughout Europe for their qualities of seriousness, belonged mainly to families who had exercised their crafts for generations. The length and rigour of apprenticeship were a guarantee of their reputation: four or five years of toil in obscurity under a recognized master were exacted from every aspirant before he could prove his own powers and attain to the skill which would allow him to set up on his own account.

Certainly there was no shortage of work. Orders were abundant, and during the sixteenth century their volume grew. After the disturbances, the destroyed altarpieces and pictures had to be replaced. No parish would pinch pennies when it came to the size and scale of the constructions which framed their altars. Sometimes, indeed, these occupied entire chapels. Orders from private persons were also considerable. Political events succeeded in slowing down the activities of patrons and collectors, but these recovered under the government of the Archduke and Archduchess Albert and Isabella.

The bourgeois of Antwerp possessed rich collections, and their studies were heaped with pictures, sculptures, intaglios, medallions, bronzes and all kinds of objets d'art, in incredible confusion, bearing witness as much to their pride of possession as to the variety of their tastes. Antwerp was crammed with works of art. This can be seen in the municipal archives, in legal documents relating to inheritances, bankruptcy proceedings, registrations of businesses and the placing of orders.

The city was run by young men. Several large concerns had at their heads youths of less than twenty, and it was these young men who made the great Flemish port the animated city it was. Audacious, all-conquering, irreverent, Antwerp defied the whole of Europe with its wealth and daring, its amusements and its amorous pursuits. Right up to the day when the Duke of Alba unleashed terror and death.

The 'Spanish fury' pillaged, sacked and burnt Antwerp from top to bottom, leaving behind it countless ruins and 10,000 dead. The slaughter only increased the hatred of the province for the occupying power. For this reason, and in order to check resistance, Alba's successor, Don John of Austria, subscribed to the Perpetual Edict decreed by the States-General, one of whose clauses demanded the departure of the Spanish troops. They left Antwerp on 26 March 1577. Three months later Rubens was born.

In Cologne, where Jan Rubens had been living with his family since 1570, the old magistrate had been chosen by Anne of Saxony, the wife of William of Orange, as her legal adviser. Since his marriage in 1561 to Maria Pypelinckx, he already had four children: Jan-Baptist[1], born in 1562; Blandine[2], born in 1564; Claire[3], born in 1565; and Hendrick[4], born in 1567. A fifth child came three years before Peter Paul, in 1574: Philip[5]. A boy, Bartholomeus, lived only a few days.

Young, handsome and enterprising, Jan Rubens became Anne's lover—she was far from shy, and her husband often left her for long periods in order to engage in warfare. The liaison had probably continued for two or three years when William the Silent discovered it. He at once ordered his brother John of Nassau to imprison this person who had come close to qualifying for the death penalty.

Maria Pypelinckx had suffered before this from her inconstant husband's escapades. Knowing him to be in danger, she set herself with obstinate courage to save him, and wrote to him incessantly at the castle of Dillenburg, where he was imprisoned and forbidden visitors; her letters contained not bitterness or recrimination but magnanimity, resignation and affection.

Some historians assert that it was Maria's desperate eagerness which saved her husband; but this seems unlikely. The Nassau family were anxious to avoid scandal—all the more as this was not Anne's first transgression. After two years Jan Rubens was released, and compulsory residence in Siegen, a small town 80 kilometres west of Cologne, was imposed on him, on pain of the forfeiture

5   Anon, *Anne of Saxony*   6   Van Mierevelt, *Prince of Orange*

of a surety. He was not allowed to return to Cologne until 1578. According to tradition it was at Siegen, on 28 June 1577, that Peter Paul Rubens was born.

The basis for the official recognition of this date as that of Rubens' birth rests, in the absence of the least bit of registry office evidence, on a single document: the mention of this date occurred for the first time in 1649, ten years after Rubens' death, beneath his portrait engraved by Jan Meyssens of Antwerp. The absence of any documentary proof has led to numerous theories, one as fanciful as the other. People have even gone so far as to suggest that his real mother was Anne of Saxony. But this is impossible if the painter really was born in 1577, for at that time Jan Rubens had been in exile at Siegen for a probable total of four years. Now a year after the beginning of this exile, and as if to seal the couple's reconciliation, Maria Pypelinckx gave birth to a son, Philip, born in 1574.

The painter himself seems to have been uncertain of the exact place of his birth. He always said he was born in Cologne, and this statement has outweighed other suggestions. (Some recent historians have even specified the Sternengasse in that city as his birthplace.) Owing to a tendency which people have to choose the most romantic of a number of possible explanations, it was rumoured that Rubens was born in Antwerp during a journey undertaken by his mother, with the purpose of settling certain questions concerning her husband's release and return to his native land. The possibility has even been bruited of a substitution of babies!

To suppport the claim that the painter was in fact the son of Anne of Saxony, its partisans emphasize the protection which he enjoyed during his childhood in spite of the fact that he was the son of an exile suspected of heresy; and his relationship, later on, with Maurice of Nassau, William's and Anne's legitimate son, and, according to this theory, his half-brother. The princess died an alcoholic. Her husband gave Jan Rubens and his family permission to return to Cologne, and it was there that Peter Paul spent his earliest years.

Paul Jamot has underlined the disturbing resemblances between the obscurity of Rubens' birth and that of Delacroix, the painter who understood and admired better than any other the work of the great Flemish Baroque painter. 'Is it not curious,' he writes[6], 'that in both cases people have been impelled to seek, in some mystery connected with their origin, the causes of the princely air which so struck their contemporaries, and which is borne out by many a portrait; and that people should tend, too, to explain in the same way certain extraordinary features of their lives?' At this point another theory arises: Peter Paul Rubens was perhaps not the son of the magistrate but the issue of a union between Maria Pypelinckx and some important person who has remained anonymous. Double adultery; double mystery. The painter would in this case have been born in Antwerp, where his mother had gone to conceal her sin on the pretext of a business journey. This would explain how it was possible for the son of an exiled commoner to become a page in the household of so exalted a person as Countess Marguerite de Ligne d'Arenberg, widow of Philip, Count of Lalaing, the former Governor of Antwerp; that is, if one can believe his nephew Philip Rubens, who in 1576 wrote a short work, *Vita Rubenii*, with a view to supplying the historian Roger de Piles with the facts. It should be added that Philip Rubens tends somewhat to glorify his uncle's memory.

On a February morning in 1587 Maria Pypelinckx and her children followed the mortal remains of Jan Rubens to the Church of St Peter in Cologne. On his tomb was placed an inscription of which the following is an extract: 'His wife, whom he gave seven children, and with whom he lived twenty-six years in concord without giving her a single cause for complaint, caused this tomb to be erected in honour of her excellent and beloved spouse.'

Was this not a way of forestalling both malicious rumours and invidious interpretations?

What did this father, hardly known, since he died when Peter Paul was ten, give to the son who was to make his name one of the most glorious in the history of art? Possibly a certain taste for daring and adventurousness. The courage, perhaps, to defy fate, and to ignore—for the eyes of a woman, for a feeling of beauty, for a moment of love and abandon—princes, judges and punishment alike. Probably Rubens never came to know anything of the faults committed by his father with a princess who loved pleasure too much. But he must have heard stories from his father of the wars that took place in his own country, and of the savage repression; and these would have haunted his childish dreams, where the turbulence of his spirit was nourished by this epic of fire and blood. Perhaps Rubens' tragic lyricism stems from this source, in the same way that Delacroix's was linked with the folly and fury of the Terror, Rouault's with the bloody excesses of the Commune, and Nicholas de Staël's with the carnage of the October Revolution in Russia. For each of them their younger days were surrounded with an atmosphere of frightfulness, violence and passion. It is as if the fears and anxieties of childhood could, in the grappling of the creator and his work, give rise to those impulses and tumults which, in the last analysis, are only imperious refusals of the decrees of fate.

Two years after the death of Jan Rubens—years of applications and entreaties which mark the course of a difficult existence—Maria Pypelinckx and her children were given permission to return to Antwerp. There, little by little, they settled into a new life. A soft, somewhat melancholy, light bathed this town, once so animated, so prosperous and so happy, and now slumbering by its canals, ravaged by war. Almost half the population had left it, and not a single ship rocked on the waters of the vast estuary or spread its sails.

The beautiful women of Antwerp and the painters who glorified them, at the same time as the merchants enriched them, were gone. In the Schilderspand, the market for pictures, there was nothing for sale, because there was no one to buy. Only with the accession to the throne of the independent Kingdom of the Netherlands of Archduke Albert and Archduchess Isabella did prosperity return. Their entry into Antwerp on 8 December 1599 was the signal of revival.

At the age of twelve Peter Paul, living with his family in the house in the Place de Meir which his mother owned jointly with her sister, entered the Latin school of Rombaut Verdonck, an excellent educator. Here the instruction in the humanities which he had received from the Jesuits in Cologne was continued. In addition he acquired or perfected Flemish, German, Spanish and French. But, as Maria Pypelinckx declared in her will of 18 December 1607, she could not provide for the needs of all her children; the adolescent was forced to discontinue his studies. It is likely that, shortly after the marriage of his sister Blandine, Peter Paul entered the service of the Countess of Lalaing. Jan Rubens' widow had crippled herself financially in order to give her daughter a proper dowry. Her son Philip, who was also obliged to earn a living, obtained a post as a private secretary in Rome.

CHAPTER TWO

Three minor masters

It is customary to seek the distinguishing marks of the man of genius in his childhood. Above Antwerp and its estuary there was limitless space; the greyish mist of early morning turned in the evening to golden dust; sails in the sunset unfurled an indescribable magic. Seaports always mean adventure, and adventure is an essential part of the first impulses of adolescence. In his walks about Antwerp the Countess de Lalaing's little page—whether accompanying his mistress to mass or attending her during her receptions and suppers—must sometimes have thought of his father's stories. What a contrast there was between those terrible events which had caused so many gaping wounds and this city where beauty was worshipped in all its forms! Although the painters had returned, and the shopkeepers had resumed their place behind their counters, and the Exchange, which when deserted by speculators and merchants was almost turned into a library, had resumed its activity—in spite of all this, Antwerp would never be the same again. This city of pleasure, luxury, riches, would continue to feel a nostalgia for its capricious freedom. The Church, victorious over the movement for reform, kept watch from now on over public morals and, if unable to regulate commerce, could at least draw to itself the second most profitable of Antwerp's activities: that of the artists who had proliferated within its walls since the beginning of the century. The Church's triumph was confirmed not only by the building of new churches and the development of the religious Orders, but even more emphatically by the volume of its commissions, whether for the embellishment of its buildings or for the further enrichment of its treasures. In addition, it now attempted to respond to the disturbing events which had shaken the city by reforming the life the city led—though the law of the Gospel can make little headway against gang-law, especially when it is in the hands of luxury-loving nobles and princes. At any rate, from now on religious rites and secular festivals were kept strictly apart.

From the beginning of the sixteenth century primitive Flemish painting, and especially in Antwerp, had mingled intimately and readily with the new trends of Renaissance art. There was as much circulation within the walls of Antwerp of cultural and artistic ideas as there was of spices from the Indies, gold from the New World, English wool and cloth, or French wines; and it was through Antwerp that the new ideas from Italy spread to the rest of the Low Countries. Ships from the Mediterranean crowded the quays: there were Italian merchants, bankers, dealers, connoisseurs—and even Italian ponces, pimps and whores. Margaret of Parma, herself very much inclined towards Italian culture, tended to impose her own tastes on the provinces she governed. And it was not only the Flemings who underwent the Italian influence; it was felt by all the foreign visitors whom Antwerp attracted. When Dürer arrived there on 2 August 1520 he had met not only Quentin Metsys, the town's most celebrated painter, but the Walloon Joachim Patinir, the Dutchmen Lucas van Leyden and Dirck Vellert, the sculptor Jean Monet from Lorraine and, from Bruges, Jan Provost who, as his compatriot Gerard David had done a few years earlier, left his own town to come and work on the banks of the Scheldt. Even before wresting from Bruges its pride of place in commerce, Antwerp had captured its position as leader in the arts.

This confluence of artists from various countries shows how far Antwerp had advanced in the first half of the sixteenth century towards being as cosmopolitan in art as it was in commerce. As the meeting point of diverse trends in painting, it played an important part in the dissemination of new ideas. These were already being put

7 Albrecht Dürer, *Antwerp Harbour*, 1520

into practice by Metsys when he began to combine the spirituality which was essentially Flemish with the delicate Italian 'sfumato': softening contours and surrounding both character and religious subjects with a new kind of charm. Metsys was followed along this line of development by Jan Gossaert and Josse van Cleve, both of them working in Antwerp; and the idea of a more refined and supple style, employing pure colours, easy and rhythmical, clearly composed, and elegantly modelled, percolated slowly into the traditionalist language of Flemish painting. With certain painters this idea gave rise to a conflict between opposing elements in the search for a style which would lay less stress on subject-matter rather than on the manner of treating it: hence these painters are known as 'mannerists'. The mannerists flourished in Antwerp, where, as in literature, they manifested in an affected and turgid style of conventional elegance their desire to break with traditional formalism even at the price of extravagance and excess. The products of an era of contradiction and change, they seemed to express in the domain of painting the fever and curiosity which were spreading through all human activity in this age of progress.

The mannerism of Antwerp was initiated by Jan de Beer, born in 1475, who in 1515 was Dean of the Guild. His colouring with its abrupt contrasts, the complex exuberance of his figures, and the virtuosity of his composition are not mere tricks but a search for a style. One cannot, unfortunately, say as much for the vast majority of the painters of his school, who were affected only superficially by the search for what was new. At the same time they can hardly be isolated from the general European movement of the first half of the

8   Pieter Brueghel the Elder, *Hunters in the Snow*, 1565

century towards individual freedom and the liberation of technique from tradition. This first 'crisis' in Flemish art was followed by many others; indeed its evolution seems to have been characterized, until the appearance of Rubens, by a series of swings between mannerism and realism, tradition and invention, the vernacular and the Italianate. If Brueghel, in presenting his extraordinary spectacle of strange figures, seems to have resolved all problems, this philosopher of shapes and movements was too individual to beget a posterity. He did, however, succeed in giving expression to the Flemish spirit and to Flemish life which Rubens was to transcend and sublimate, and finally absorb into the Baroque genius of his own artistic expression.

Flemish as Brueghel was—and he was admirably, even tyrannically so—the spectacle of the everyday life of his country did not blind him to what was taking place in the great world beyond it. His art was opposed, certainly, to fashionable Italianism; but he went far beyond simple folk-painting, and in fact achieved what the Italians, whose country he visited about 1552-53, had introduced into the painting of his time; the sense of space and the capacity to integrate living beings into it. But he opposed the merely decorative effects and the exuberance and turbulence of the mannerists; he imposed limits on himself, whereas they refused them and questioned everything: tradition, established convictions, the very spirit of art itself. Nevertheless it was he who was far-seeing, not they; despite their ambitions they never found a style. What links Brueghel with the mannerists is their spirit of humanist enquiry; and this at last had its result, for in the long run the Italian influence on the direction taken by Flemish painting was slight, and mannerism was finally seen to have been a momentary response to the confusion of the age which gave it birth *(Pl. 8)*.

The dramatic events which had taken place in Antwerp caused the exodus of its painters, who emigrated to the northern provinces and worked out the phases of mannerism and the influence of Brueghel's realism. The separation between Calvinist North and Catholic South did not, however, affect them for long. Reconstruction was a matter of urgency and, for the time being at least, physical facts were more important than ideas. The fury of the people had wrought havoc; the works of art which filled the churches had especially provoked the Calvinists. The Counter-Reformation attached great importance to their restoration, and insisted on giving the altars a triumphal aspect; heavy and pretentious, these were to embody paintings of vast dimensions.

Thus it was that there arose a school, or rather a movement of painters, to whom these ambitious schemes were confided. Since it was based on a religious grouping in Antwerp, from 1572 onwards, of all those painters who had been to Rome, its members were known as 'Romanists'. It included not only painters but collectors, scholars, ecclesiastics and travellers of artistic interests. Despite its name, the confraternity of Romanists was much closer to traditional Flemish painting than to 'Italianizing' tendencies. 'They seemed,' wrote Leo van Puyvelde[7], 'to glory in magnifying beyond all measure the paintings of the primitives, without themselves retaining their moderation and sensitivity, or their realism and brilliance of colour. They limited themselves to adding to the primitive style a sort of classicism in their grouping of figures and choice of colouring.' It was these painters who were important in the artistic life of Antwerp when Peter Paul Rubens began to take shape as a painter; and it was therefore natural that he should turn towards them.

Maria Pypelinckx's ambitions for her son were encouraged by the gracefulness of his appearance. She had succeeded, despite his father's behaviour, in getting him a place as page to one of the most important ladies in Antwerp; she saw him already as a magistrate like Jan Rubens, or a prominent merchant. We do not know whether his stay with the Countess de Lalaing was cut short by the bad examples he witnessed in her service. Isaac Bullart[8] assures us that Rubens could not 'put up with the licentiousness of this court life …'

It is not known why he turned towards painting, or whether he really had a natural aptitude for it. De Piles, who follows Philip Rubens, claims that the decision, which according to the artist was made 'in order to teach himself for his own pleasure', was motivated mainly by his mother's financial straits and by 'the losses she had incurred as a result of the wars'. De Piles' *Abrégé de la vie des peintres*[9], published in 1699, which covers much of the ground of the *Vita Rubenii*, cannot be taken too literally. De Piles bases his statements on the testimony of contemporaries who knew Rubens; on the other hand he relies also on such doubtful accounts as those in Baglioni and de Bellori's *Vies des peintres*. Nor is Joachim von Sandrart's *Teutsche Academie der edelen Bau-, Bild- und Mahlerey-Künste*, published in two volumes (1675 and 1679), any more reliable. It is necessary to be cautious in assigning a definite origin to Rubens' vocation.

His entry into the studio of Tobias Verhaecht is mentioned only very late, and without any specific date, first by Jan Meyssens on his portrait engraving of the painter (1649), and then by Sandrart. Philip Rubens, however, says nothing about it, and attributes to his uncle only two masters: Adam van Noort and Octave van Veen—still without giving any definite date. Roger de Piles, without citing his sources, says that Rubens worked for four years under the first of them, and for the same period under the second.

Fromentin, who appears to have allowed his imagination to run away with him, describes Adam van Noort as 'The only painter of that epoch who had remained Flemish when no one else in Flanders had done so.' After this appraisal, he continues: 'He possessed neither culture nor manners, nor elegance, nor dignity of bearing, nor amenableness, nor steadiness; but to compensate for these failings he had real and vivid gifts ... He was a man of many talents who could succeed at anything. Possibly he was an ignoramus, but he was somebody ...'

Octave van Veen, who Latinized his name into Otto Venius, had arrived from Leyden to establish himself in Antwerp in 1590. Rubens

9 Otto Venius, *The Painter and his Family*

seems to have worked in his studio from 1594 to 1598, the date of his admittance into the Guild of St Luke.

What did he learn from his two masters? Little of painting, probably, since neither Verhaecht nor Van Noort nor Van Veen had a style which was capable of imposing itself on a young apprentice. What they did was to acquaint him with what are called the 'rudiments'. They set him, simply, to learn Antwerp: the mind and soul of the city which his genius would one day assume like a cloak. They pointed out to him its excellences and its failings, its tastes, its foibles, and its desires, as all these were reflected in the people—prelates, princes, collectors and women of fashion—who visited them to see or to judge the works in their studios. And their studios, hardly ever empty of such visitors, were microcosms of this city which simmered with curiosity and liveliness: the meeting-place and sometimes the battlefield of so many tendencies, currents of thought, influences and ideas. What Antwerp was, each painter's studio was too: a place intensely occupied with its own affairs, and at the same time intensely concerned with what was going on outside it.

As far as one can surmise, then—for there are no documents relating to the dates of Rubens' apprenticeships—he stayed at Van Veen's until he was twenty-one. He was to owe to him as a painter no more than Delacroix owed later to Guérin, or Manet to Couture; what he learnt from this teacher he could have learnt from anyone. But, like Guérin and Couture, Van Veen was a man of his time: he reflected its fashions, its tastes, its impulses, curiosities and contradictions, and these are transmitted more readily to a pupil through a master of undistinguished talent than through a genius. Geniuses, indeed, do not have disciples, only imitators. For Rubens, who was in no hurry to reveal himself or to produce finished works of art, and whose first pictures are still a matter of guesswork, it was more important to belong to the school of Antwerp than to follow in the footsteps of a master. And to be loyal to the Flemish tradition and at the same time feel attracted by Italian importations of style was not merely to study painting but life itself.

Rubens was elected to the title of Master in the Guild of St Luke in 1598, according to the records of that body; from then on he was free to sell his own works. He was not rich, and Maria Pypelinckx often had difficulty in making ends meet. Peter Paul did not appear, however, to be in any hurry to work and make money. Probably he decided that his apprenticeship had not yet been completed, that he needed to see other things besides Antwerp, its painters and their pictures. The dream which haunted him was the dream of every young painter of his time, and particularly of those in Antwerp. It was to go to Italy.

Italy had exalted some and inspired others, but for many Flemish painters the Italian influence was dangerous; no sooner had they come

10   Hans Holbein, *Danse macabre*

near Italian art than they lost their own character and plunged into
pastiche. Only a strong personality like Brueghel's was capable of
borrowing from the Italians only what could be used by the Flemish
temperament, Flemish intentions, the Flemish view of art; assimilat-
ing the foreign while remaining itself. Many Flemish painters simply
lost themselves without ever arriving at a solution to the problem
which occupied them most—the integration of figures in space.
'We would cudgel our brains,' wrote Leo van Puyvelde, 'to achieve a
little spaciousness in the settings in which our figures were placed.'
Notwithstanding this, a visit to Italy was part of the apprenticeship
—later it would be called the 'equipment'—of every young artist.
At the time of the political troubles several painters from Flanders
actually set up house in Italy and remained there until peace was
restored. However they brought nothing back which was capable
of changing their contemporaries' attitude towards Italian painting.
Probably their attitude can be explained as an inferiority complex
about Italian painters; at all events there was no personality among
them powerful enough to settle the question.

It is stated by Sandrart that the painter told him that, during the
period of his apprenticeship in Antwerp, he had made copies of

Holbein's *Danse Macabre*, of Dürer, and of a painting by Tobias Stimmer. In her will, Maria Pypelinckx, having left several portraits of herself to her sons, writes: 'All the other pictures, which are very fine ones, belong to Peter, who painted them.' But the only work of Rubens' youth which has come down to us is the *Portrait of a young Savant*, also known as *L'Horloger*. Painted in oils on a small copper plate (21.6 × 14.6 cm.), it is in the collection of Mr and Mrs Jack Linsky of New York. The portrait is inscribed on the back: PETRUS PAULUS RUBENS PI (NXIT). The date, 1597, and the age of the model, are on the portrait itself: A: MDLXXXXVII, AETATIS XXVI. It is possible that the first inscription is not in Rubens' own hand. The second has sometimes caused this work to be known as *L'Homme de vingt-six ans*. The model in this half-length portrait holds in his right hand a set-square and another instrument, possibly a compass; with his right hand he lifts a chain from which hangs another, unidentified, instrument.

This painting has been studied not only by its discoverer, Professor Rudolf Oldenbourg, but by W. Bode and Christopher Norris.[10] Were it not proved a genuine Rubens, hardly anything but the intensity of the model's look and the elegance of the gesture of the hand would call attention to it. A number of painters who were in Antwerp at this time could have done this unremarkable portrait. André de Hevesy[11] compares it with another portrait of a man in a Swiss collection, and, having shown striking similarities between them, attributes the Swiss portrait without hesitation to Rubens. He also identifies the sitter, according to the heraldic devices which appear on the portrait, as Claude-Adolphe de Maubouhans, Treasurer-General of Burgundy. This seems, however, a little far-fetched.

More convincing than the *Portrait of a young Savant* is a work discovered shortly after the Second World War by Leo van Puyvelde[12], called *Portrait of a young Painter*, in which the great Belgian art-historian is inclined to see a Rubens self-portrait. Long attributed to Pedro Orrente, the painting belongs to the J. G. Johnson collection in the Philadelphia Museum of Art. It is known that the future painter of the *Coup de Lance (Pl. 69)* did work on self-portraiture at this time, since a self-portrait by the young Rubens is mentioned in an inventory taken after the death of the Antwerp painter Abraham Matthys in 1649.

It is a remarkable canvas, and M. van Puyvelde justly admires 'the fading in and out of yellow and pink in the highlights of the flesh-tints; the bluish tones of the skin between the lighter colours and the brown shadows; the red in the shaded parts of the ear, and a peculiar treatment of the eyes.' According to him these characteristic signs can be found in a work of somewhat later date: the *Portrait of Francesco IV Gonzaga*[13] (not Vincenzo II, as he has it) in the Kunsthistorisches Museum in Vienna, which has been recognized to be a fragment of the great *Adoration of the Trinity by the Gonzaga Family* painted in 1604-5 at Mantua, and since broken up into smaller pieces.

After obtaining his Mastership, Rubens worked for another two years in Antwerp before deciding on his departure. On 8 May 1600 he obtained a certificate of good character and health—which is preserved in the communal archives—and set out for Italy.

Rubens' main aim was to perfect himself in painting by contact with classical art and with the work of the Renaissance masters; but he also hoped to find in Italy remunerative employment which would gain him prosperity and reputation. It is probable that his own position in relation to the disagreements, inhibitions and scruples of his compatriots took second place in his mind. Without doubt he had begun to produce work of his own before leaving Antwerp, but too little is known of his youthful productions to be of use to us.

CHAPTER THREE

The Italian campaign

'Go, Rubens! I salute your art which promises new splendours under our skies! Go to Italy and enquire of Nature, who is deaf to all but the voice of Genius! Go and pursue, for the perfection of your skill as a painter, the studies which the great Masters pursued before you!'

With such lyrical effusions, a certain J. F. Boussard, registrar of the canton of Nivelles, began in 1840 his description of the painter's journey from Antwerp to Rome, entitled *Les Voyages Pittoresques et Politiques de Pierre-Paul Rubens depuis 1600, rédigés sur les Manuscrits de la Bibliothèque de Bourgogne.* According to him—though he unfortunately gives no sources—the painter travelled through Burgundy before entering Franche-Comté, where he spent a week at Arbois as the guest of the nephews of Mercurin de Gattinara, one of Charles V's chancellors. At Besançon he went to pay homage to Archbishop Ferdinand de Rye, chaplain to the Archduke Albert and Isabella; then he travelled towards Basle to admire the works of Holbein, whom Boussard calls 'a zealous and faithful imitator of nature'. The 'formidable peaks of the Alps' had a deep effect on Rubens; he had, indeed, 'no first-hand knowledge of the smallest mountain range'; and these, 'heaped up like ocean waves and rising with an extraordinary strength of projection' were calculated, if one is to believe our registrar, to astound. At La Novaleze, the first Piedmontese village, Rubens descended into Italy and set course for Padua and Venice.

Where did J. F. Boussard obtain his facts? The 'Library of Burgundy' has never existed, and no manuscripts relating to the painter's journey have ever been brought to light in any of the establishments or institutions belonging to the former Duchy. Further, we do not know on what documents Boussard is relying when he talks of the excellent relations that existed between Rubens and persons in high places, and which caused him to appear already as a person of importance on this journey. It would be absurd to give any credit to such allegations were it not for the fact that as soon as he arrived in Italy, where he knew no one, the young Fleming found himself possessed of the title and duties of court painter to the Duke of Mantua, Vincenzo Gonzaga, a great patron and collector. This was an enviable position for a newcomer and a foreigner to occupy.

'I served the Gonzaga family for many years,' wrote Rubens to the learned Nicolas Peiresc; 'and while I was young the delights of a stay in that part of Italy were very much to my taste.'

The unexpected promotion of the painter might at first sight look like a supporting argument for the theory of Rubens' illustrious origins, which would have justified this high calling. The *Vita Rubenii* assures us that a nobleman of the Mantuan court, meeting Rubens in Venice, took him to his master in order to place him in the post of court painter. It is best to accept this explanation for want of more precise information. Certain circumstances make it seem a likely one. The Duke of Mantua was in Venice from 16 to 22 July 1600, and Rubens is likely to have been there at the same time. It is true that the almost daily reports of Vincenzo Gonzaga's agent in Venice, which are now in the Ducal archives in Mantua, say nothing of the painter's residence in Venice, nor of any meeting between him and the Duke or any of his retinue during this period. But it is also possible that the Archduke, who thought very highly of Rubens, recommended him to his friend Duke Gonzaga.

The duties of court painter included, by tradition, various obligations: the execution of portraits of the prince and his family; the copying of famous works of which he desired to have replicas in his gallery; and finally the undertaking of the decoration of various

rooms of halls in the palace. Vincenzo Gonzaga, a gambler, a quar-
reller, a pious believer and a keen pursuer of women, was especially
anxious to collect portraits of beautiful women. He had been married
twice, once to a Farnese and then to a Medici, and had turned his
court into a meeting-place for artists, musicians, actors, idlers,
roisterers and frequenters of gambling-houses and brothels. His
mania for luxury and his generosity as a patron were as famous as his
large number of mistresses.

Mantua itself was both severe and attractive. The Ducal palace,
built in the thirteenth century but several times remodelled, had a
noble air. The Gonzagas were well known for their taste and patro-
nage. Gianfrancesco I collected round him both artists and scholars,
and his son Francesco sent for Brunelleschi, Donatello and Pisanello.
Ludovico Gonzaga, his grandson, proved to be the classic type of
enlightened Renaissance despot: it was he who invited Mantegna,
who was to leave a number of masterpieces in Mantua. Vincenzo
Gonzaga was worthy of his predecessors. Thanks to him Rubens
found himself in a centre of culture and art where the works of
Italian masters abounded: Titian, Correggio, Raphael, Tintoretto,
Veronese. This was not Rubens' first contact with the art which so
preoccupied his compatriots; but he could now see and study it in a
different climate and a different light. The paintings looked quite
different under the transparent blue sky of Mantua from what he had
seen in the greyness of Antwerp.

Life was pleasant. The Duke entertained a great deal. He enjoyed
elaborate festivities, and Rubens regarded this new social milieu with
the same sharp curiosity he had shown in the studios of Antwerp.
The Italians were charming and hospitable, a little frivolous perhaps
and wanting in moderation. They loved pleasure, luxury and beauty.
Their fondness for women was at least equal to that of the Flemish,
though they expressed it somewhat differently. Vincenzo had a
weakness for actresses, and it is possible that Rubens painted their
portraits along with those of the Ducal family. There was, however,

11   Nattier, *The Marriage of Maria de' Medici*

another Fleming, Frans Pourbus, working at the court of Mantua, like Rubens, and it was his job to carry out this work: portraits were his speciality.

Nearly all Rubens historians have made a point of stating that the Duke took his painter on 5 October 1600 to the wedding by proxy of his sister-in-law Maria de' Medici to Henri IV of France, under the dome of Sta Maria del Fiore in Florence. The King was at this time warring in Savoy, where he was said to spend his time mainly in 'wanton and excessive behaviour'. This 'meeting' between the

Flemish painter and the Florentine princess who, twenty years later, commissioned the series of masterpieces in the Galerie du Luxembourg, is a romantic element in the story which should probably be abandoned despite Peiresc's letter to Rubens of 27 October 1622: 'I observed with pleasure that you had been present at the wedding of the Queen-Mother at Sta Maria del Fiore, and that you had been inside the banqueting-hall.' This sentence seems in fact to refer to the impression of precision which the Luxembourg painting gives, rather than to Rubens' actual presence at the ceremony *(Pl. 11)*.

There is no proof, in point of fact, that Rubens was at Mantua before the beginning of October 1600. The Duke and Duchess had been travelling for several weeks at that time, and none of the reports sent daily from his Duchy to Vincenzo Gonzaga mentions the painter's arrival. The journey, which took the Duke from his estates of Montferrat, east of Turin, to Florence and Genoa, did not end until the end of December, when his wife Eleonora de' Medici returned, having accompanied her sister, Henri IV's bride, to Marseilles. For more than three months there is nothing—not a letter nor a report—to show that Rubens was either travelling with his patron or at Mantua. Some have inferred from this that Rubens arrived in Mantua only after the Duke's return during the last days of the year; but on this point there is uncertainty.

We know nothing more, either about Rubens' life at the court of Mantua or about the work on which he was engaged, until July 1601, when Vincenzo Gonzaga, who was preparing to assist the Emperor Rudolph in his war against the Turks, sent Rubens to Rome in order to copy some paintings by the masters for his palace. One of the first documents referring to this is a letter of 18 July 1601 in which the Duke recommends to the Grand Elector of the Conclave, Cardinal Alessandro Montaldo, 'Peter Paul, a Fleming, my painter, whom I am sending to you to carry out the copying of certain works of art ...' The prelate's reply, dated 15 August, confirms Rubens' arrival in Rome.

There also exists a letter of 8 June, in which the Archduke Albert informs his representative in Rome, Jean Richardot, that he is ordering from his young compatriot certain paintings intended for the Church of Santa Croce in Gerusalemme. Duke Gonzaga would hardly have been able to refuse the 'loan' of his young painter to the Archduke. But to put the Cardinal off the scent and allow it to be thought that it was for himself that Rubens had gone to work in Rome seems to have been irresistible. As for Rubens, he was certainly capable of serving two masters.

Albert, Regent of the Netherlands, sixth son of the German Emperor Maximilian II, had been brought up at the court of Madrid and was intended from his earliest youth for an ecclesiastical career. At the age of eighteen he had been made Cardinal of the Santa Croce in Gerusalemme in Rome, and then Archbishop of Toledo; but in 1599 he was absolved of his religious vows in order to marry Isabella, Infanta of Spain, to whom her father, Philip II, had entrusted the government of the Netherlands. It was for his church in Rome, whose protector he remained, that Albert commissioned Rubens to carry out three paintings. They were finished in January 1602. It is not known what Rubens did in Rome apart from this work between August 1601 and his return to Mantua eight months later.

When Vincenzo Gonzaga returned from his military expedition he complained of the prolonged absence of his court painter. Richardot had to write him a long letter (26 January 1602) to obtain his permission for Rubens to finish the paintings and fix them in position. Rubens did not return to Mantua until April.

These paintings, or more exactly this triptych, comprises *The Finding of the True Cross by St Helena* flanked by the *Crown of Thorns* and the *Raising of the Cross*. After many wanderings these are now in the chapel of the Hospice du Petit-Paris at Grasse, a legacy from their former owner, a local collector, M. Peyrolle.

After years of being covered with dirt, these pictures have now been cleaned and can be seen. They appear deliberately Italian in

12 *Homer*. Drawing after an antique gold coin

13 *Alexander*. Drawing after an antique gold coin

technique and spirit. The figures are placed, with a sense of drama, on backgrounds whose colouring reveals golden tints, reminiscent of Venetian painting, applied with great ease and skill. But it is clear from these pictures that Rubens was less the disciple of the Flemish 'Italianate' painters than an admirer of the artists then fashionable in Rome. This is neither pastiche nor copying; it is an assimilation. Rubens is playing at painting in the spirit of the masters of his own time, but he is speaking, at it were, directly to them, without intermediaries or complications. These vast compositions contain little which is personal and do not stand out particularly from the ecclesiastical painting of the time. It is in their colour distribution and intensity—very skilfully determined—that they are most original. 'Here already are the firm tints that will remain pecu-

41

liar to the master: the dark red of the curtain in *The Finding of the True Cross*, and the blackness with which the brownish yellow of the saint's cloak contrasts,' writes Leo van Puyvelde.[14] The composition itself is heavy and congested; the figures disproportionately large. This is a treatment typical of Rubens, though here it appears to be lacking in scale.

This triptych can be compared with the *Entombment* and *Susanna and the Elders* in the Borghese Gallery in Rome; their style is similar and they have other characteristics in common.

The *Entombment* was for a long time attributed to Van Dyck, and it was F. M. Haberditzl[15] who first pointed out the connexion between this work and the paintings of Santa Croce: they share the same slightly squat figures, with similar faces and identical postures. In terms of style the comparison is even more convincing: as in the Roman triptych, the overall brownish tones are here and there relieved by brighter tints, such as the fine red of St John's robe, the

14   *The Entombment*

red-gold hair of Mary Magdalene and the greenish colour of her cloak. These are connected with certain reddish reflections in the flesh-tints. Besides this, there is the lighting—mechanical but effective—which steadies the semicircular composition of the figures round Christ, in the 'Italian' manner; this, together with certain weaknesses of form—particularly the foreshortening of Christ's thighs—is a quite convincing demonstration of Rubens' manner of the period. The very careful 'reproduction' of the sarcophagus bears witness to his preoccupation with archaeology, as do many of his Italian studies of the antique; there is little doubt that this was drawn from nature.

This picture, which is part of the original collection of the Borghese Gallery, may have been acquired by Cardinal Scipione Borghese, the famous patron and connoisseur, with whom Rubens was in contact in Rome.

Although *Susanna and the Elders* also contains similarities to Rubens' paintings of this period, its precise date is less certain. It is possible that this work, whose subject Rubens worked on a number of times, was in fact executed during his second visit to Rome about 1608.

In April 1602 the painter returned to Mantua. His activities are unknown until the spring of the following year when the Duke placed him in charge of a shipment of presents to the Spanish King, to whom he was certainly under an obligation like the rest of the Italian princes, even if he was not his vassal. These presents, which were intended to promote good relations with the court of Madrid, included, for the King himself, a coach and horses; eleven arquebuses, 'six of them in whalebone, and six with rifled bores'; and a rock crystal vase filled with perfume. For the Duke of Lerma, the Prime Minister, there were 'all the paintings, together with a large silver vessel of perfume and some golden vessels'. Other presents were sent to the Countess of Lemos, the King's favourite, and to her secretary Pedro Franqueza.

That a foreign painter only twenty-five years old should have been entrusted with such a mission shows how highly the Duke valued him. Admittedly the Duke knew that Rubens was in high favour with Archduke Albert, so that sending him to the Archduke's uncle, the King of Spain, was a calculated move. But in any case it was not, as has sometimes been supposed, a political mission.

Rubens' letters to Annibale Chieppio, Duke Gonzaga's secretary, are full of information and sound opinions about the court of Madrid, the King, his ministers and his entourage. They are also interesting because of the light they throw upon the character of the painter, revealing his bitterness at his own lack of personal liberty, his concern with financial questions (the Duke allowed him to go short of money in a way which hurt his feelings), but also the importance he attached to himself—not, perhaps, because he thought so highly of himself, but because he was imbued with his mission and wished to bring it to as successful an issue as possible.

Rubens left Mantua on 5 March 1603 and travelled through Florence and Pisa to embark at Leghorn. When he arrived at Valladolid where the King of Spain and his court were, he found that the copies of the Raphael paintings done by Pietro Facchetti had been damaged by rain. 'Although the canvases themselves had been protected by sheets of zinc covered by a double thickness of waxed canvas and packed in wooden packing-cases, they were spoilt and damaged by the torrential rains which we had for twenty-five days—a thing unheard of in Spain,' wrote Rubens to Chieppio in a state of vexation.[16]

What could be done about it? At first Rubens refused to restore the pictures himself, 'because my principles forbid me to mingle my work with anyone else's, however great a man he may be'; but in the end he agreed, although the Duke of Mantua's representative at the Spanish court, Annibale Iberti, who referred to Rubens contemptuously as 'Il Fiamengo', continually irritated his pride in petty ways. He added several canvases of his own to the presents.

15   *Portrait of the Duke of Lerma*

Rubens was apt to lose his temper and kick against the traces; but these events were also opportunities for him to show his firmness of character without departing from courtesy, still less from his deference towards his employer. This did not prevent him from lashing out with his pen at Iberti who, in contravention of the procedure laid down for the solemn presentation of the gifts to the King of Spain, had failed to introduce Rubens to him. Rubens showed himself, understandably, embittered at this treatment.

The tone of his letters foreshadows the future diplomat: courtly but proud, gifted with powers of reflection and judgment, clear-headed, perspicacious, with great psychological penetration, an alert eye, a sharp intelligence, and a prompt repartee. This man knew

16   *St Jude*   17   *St Simon*

what he was, what he represented and what he wanted; and at the age of twenty-five that is no common thing.

In the end he restored the pictures so skilfully that neither the King nor the Duke of Lerma nor anyone else suspected the damage they had suffered. It is true that 'the paintings, thanks to good retouching, looked very fair, and the accidents they had undergone even gave them the appearance of older works. The Duke took them for originals, for the most part, at least; and he did not, I believe, have the smallest suspicion about them; nor did we, on our part, find it necessary to insist on their authenticity.'[17] There is a certain maliciousness in this humour.

In Valladolid and Madrid, at the Escorial and the Duke of Lerma's palace, Rubens was able to see large collections of paintings: 'numbers of splendid Titians and Raphaels,' he wrote to Chieppio, '...whose quality and quantity literally petrified me. As for modern paintings,' he added, 'there is not one worth looking at.'[18]

While in Spain, he was commissioned to paint a series of Apostles' Busts, preserved in the Prado *(Pls. 16, 17)*, as well as several portraits, including that of the Duke of Lerma which is in the collection of the Countess Valdelagrava in Madrid *(Pl. 15)*. The Louvre and the Weimar Museum have detailed studies, in which can already be seen the balance, the sureness of form and the vigour of his daring conception of the equestrian portrait. The sitter, who seems to contemplate the spectator from the height of his mount, has great bearing. Rubens made use of cunning short cuts to accentuate the plastic importance of the whole, which is painted with great spirit. This magnificent painting is the first known in which the artist displays, with tremendous confidence, the personal qualities which he was later to develop.

After a year in Spain he returned to Mantua. Vincenzo Gonzaga cherished the idea of Rubens' returning by way of Paris in order to paint some portraits of beautiful women. He wished, as he wrote to Carlo Rossi, his deputy in France (11 February 1604), to set

18   *The Apostles, c.* 1605

19　*Baptism of Christ, c.* 1605

aside a room in which he might gather together 'portraits of all the most beautiful women in the world, both nobles and commoners'. Rubens set himself to escape these 'base and vulgar employments', at all costs, as unworthy of him. His letter to Chieppio justifying his refusal, with all its pride, is the letter of a most accomplished courtier, well-used to serving and dealing with princes.

From the first weeks of 1604 until November 1605 the painter worked in Mantua. To show his satisfaction with his services the Duke made him, on 2 June 1604, a pensioner with a salary of 400 ducats per annum, payable quarterly from 24 May.

During this period his protector asked him to carry out three important works for the church of the Jesuits. These, according to Dr Gustav Glück[19], constituted a triptych: the *Transfiguration*, now in the Nancy Museum; the *Baptism of Christ*[20], which belongs to the Antwerp Museum; and the *Holy Trinity worshipped by Vincenzo Gonzaga and his Family*. In 1797 French troops removed this canvas

20 *Head of an old Woman*

from the church and cut it into pieces; the main fragment, in two pieces, and a smaller fragment are in the Ducal Palace in Mantua; others are in the collection of Dr Ludwig Burchard in London, in the Museo Civico in Verona, and in the Kunsthistorisches Museum, Vienna. Two sketches for the portraits are in Stockholm Museum.

If the *Transfiguration*, which has been much retouched, and the *Baptism of Christ*, also heavily restored, are confused works, full of large gesticulating figures, lacking balance, and with sadly altered colours, the main fragments of the *Holy Trinity* preserved at Mantua show a clarity and orderliness of composition, painted with the usual Rubens dash and spirit, but with an overall sense of values which is underlined by the use of vivid, audacious, typically Rubens colouring. Here Rubens is visibly dissociating himself from influences and fashions, and affirming himself. Neither Italian nor Flemish conventions of technique suit his temperament. His personality, held in check in the *Transfiguration* and the *Baptism of Christ* by the formulas of the period, seems to burst out in the canvas representing the Gonzagas, whose likenesses are executed with vigour and authority, as the *Portrait of Francesco IV* in Vienna proves. Was it really the same man who painted this splendid decorative composition and the Antwerp *Baptism* with its chaotic appearance and its over-emphasis, and its Christ inspired by that of Raphael in the Loggia of the Vatican? The operatic *Transfiguration* is also inspired by Raphael. This masterpiece of ecclesiastical conventionalism is surprising, coming as it does from the brush which, a few years later, was to produce the extraordinary *Raising of the Cross* of Antwerp. Nevertheless, on examination these two works reveal, behind the extravagant gestures and rhetoric, a robustness, a grandeur and a dramatic power which announce a master. There is a preparatory drawing for the *Baptism of Christ* in the Louvre *(Pl. 19)*.

In the same year, 1605, the Duke of Mantua was asked by the Emperor Rudolph to order Rubens to copy two works by Correggio belonging to the Gonzagas. A letter from the Duke to his representative at the Emperor's court shows that these copies were carried out at once 'by the hand of the Fleming' and sent to the Emperor who received them, in Prague, on 24 October.

Rubens' stay in Genoa is not well known. It occurred probably in 1605-6, and its purpose was, very likely, the painting of the portrait of the Duke of Mantua's banker. The painter certainly signed and dated at Genoa in 1606 the *Portrait of Brigida Spinola* (coll. Mrs Bankes, Kingston Lacy, Dorsetshire), whose vigorous execution, freshness of colouring and ease of composition would answer in no uncertain terms anyone who doubted its attribution to Rubens.

At this date Brigida Spinola was engaged to be married to the Doge Doria, and it is possible that Rubens made several portraits of her. A number of representations of this attractive lady were put up for sale during the last century, or attracted attention in galleries in London and Berlin. The portrait which belongs to Mrs Bankes can be compared with another in the same collection, of the Marchesa Grimaldi with her dwarf: both of these came from the Palazzo Grimaldi in Genoa.

No doubt Rubens painted other society portraits during his stay in Genoa. They were for a long time attributed to Van Dyck, although their style is characteristic of his famous predecessor. Supporters of the theory which attributes them to Van Dyck appear not to have noticed that Genoese fashions of 1605-6 had changed by the time of Van Dyck's visit fifteen years later. Among these portraits are the *Lady of the Durazzo Family*, in the Strasbourg Museum; the *Bust of an old Woman* in the royal palace in Genoa; and a *Portrait of an old woman seated next to a young girl standing*, which is in a private collection in Berlin. In these pictures the artist breaks with the convention of the set portrait by lengthening the profiles and lending them added elegance through the use of the short cuts already visible

21 *Hero and Leander, c.* 1606

in the portrait of the Duke of Lerma, and which he may have borrowed from the El Grecos which he had closely studied in the Escorial. By introducing into these compositions columns and balustrades he adds to the nobility and grandeur of the portraits.

On 26 September 1606, Paolo Agostino Spinola complained that Rubens, who was in Rome, had not completed his portrait of Spinola and his wife. It seems, therefore, that Rubens had interrupted his visit to Genoa in order to travel to Rome, where, in addition to making copies of paintings for Vincenzo Gonzaga, he was looking for work. He was there several months earlier, for he had been asking, through Chieppio, for money from the Duke. There was some question, at this time, of his accompanying the Duke to Flanders, but the journey was never made. There was a very good reason for Rubens to spend most of the year 1606 in Rome, and to neglect his work in Genoa: he was ambitious for the commission to execute the large painting with which the Oratorian Fathers wished to decorate the high altar of their Church of Sta Maria in Valicella.

The *Hero and Leander* in the Dresden Gallery can, from its style, be attributed to Rubens in this period *(Pl. 21)*. This mythological composition, which, before undergoing a succession of adventures, belonged to Rembrandt, is dramatically conceived and full of power and movement. The *Landscape with the Shipwreck of Aeneas* in the Berlin Museums, which is no less tragic, certainly belongs to the same period. This point can be proved by comparing the two paintings.

Although the scene represented in the Berlin painting was at Porto Venere, near Spezia, the picture is much more than a simple descriptive landscape. Its real subject is the battle of the elements, expressed with extraordinary spirit and freedom, and emphasized by the curved movement of the composition: the curves of the hills, the path and the bridge, whose undulations are echoed by those of the tree bent by the storm and the rocks onto which the ship has run. This is Baroque expressionism at its height. The contrasts between the light and the shadows, the unleashed hurricane and the flatness of the sea, the heavy storm-clouds and the calm horizon, carry the eye beyond the mere anecdote into high drama: the drama of nature, which overshadows—as it does in the *Aeneid* itself—that of the shipwrecked navigator.

The colours are brought into harmony by means of a brown pigment laid on generously and relieved by brighter spots of luminous yellow and pink contrasting with the sombre violence of the storm. The sky, obscured by long clouds fringed with brightness, dominate the middle ground, which is more luminous. The execution is rapid, decisive and virile.

Genoa inspired Rubens to carry out some architectural drawings; plans, sections and elevations of its most important palaces. He was to publish these in May 1622 in Antwerp, under the title *Palazzi di Genova*, with a dedication to Don Carlo Grimaldi. In it the painter shows, over and above his lively interest in Italian ornamentation and Italian palazzi, which one can observe in his paintings, a genuine knowledge of architecture.

'I do not know whom to apply to in order to obtain the favour I seek, if not to your Highness, thanks to whom I have already

22 *The Prophet Joel*   23 *The Prophet Jeremiah*

received one of the same kind. I refer to the four months' honorarium so promptly paid me by your Highness. Time has passed quickly, and I am again owed for four months: from 1 April to 1 August...'[21]

'I am vexed by his Most Serene Highness's decision which commands me to return to Mantua at such short notice that it cannot be obeyed. I cannot, as a matter of fact, think of leaving Rome at such short notice, owing to some considerable works which I freely confess to you I was forced to undertake after a whole summer of application to my art, because I could not honourably maintain a house and two servants in Rome with only the 140 crowns which are all that I have received from Mantua during my absence. Besides which, this is the most happy opportunity imaginable of taking advantage of my skill and thirst for work.

'It is the ornamenting of the high altar of the new church of the Oratorian Fathers, Sta Maria in Vallicella, the most renowned and fashionable of all the churches in Rome...'[22]

'The letter of credit for fifty crowns, payable on sight, is to hand. The lateness of its arrival by a few days is of small importance, since it has in no wise incommoded me; indeed your Highness shows too much kindness in thus honouring his servant with confidences and excuses in respect of such trifling matters...'[23]

Such was the character of Rubens. Proud, ambitious, authoritative and sure of himself: this was the painter, whose mastery was asserting itself, and whose reputation was growing. Supple, even cunning, certainly clever, plagued by money problems, and anxious to maintain his place with honour: this was the man, a zealous servant, a functionary and a diplomat. The two sides are complementary; they correspond and mingle. Rubens needed money, servants, work, freedom; he needed everything that might establish his talent, his audience and the idea of his own importance. One can imagine him, at this time, in the flower of his young manhood: handsome, elegant, well-built, attractive to women, eloquent and persuasive. His works had had some success; his protector was flattered by his growing reputation; admirers were collecting round him. He now felt capable of undertaking great works which would enable him even more than the *Holy Trinity* to make use of his prodigious dramatic gifts and the knowledge of composition and colour he had acquired in Italy. Sure of the precise nature of his powers and his gifts, he could now take his place among the best artists in Rome. And since he was well aware that more than talent was needed to be in the forefront of his profession, he had decided to let nothing pass that might serve his purpose. Slowly and patiently the figure of Rubens was taking shape.

He breathed in the air and scents of the city, appreciating its wit, its fickleness, its subtlety. He liked the street shows, the amusements of the aristocracy, the ostentation of the Church and the beauty of the women—courtesans and duchesses alike. He was, in fact, an eclectic, studying the antique; Mantegna whose work he had known well since he had been in Mantua; Michelangelo; Titian; Leonardo. Caravaggio, whose ruthless realism was beginning to scandalize people, interested him. Against them all, he measured his own potentialities. He did not get excited; he informed himself; he analysed, studied, observed. He also had an opportunity to be of service to his protector in giving him his opinion on the paintings and stucco work of the Palazzo Capo di Ferro, which the Duke wished to acquire for his son Fernandino, recently promoted Cardinal.

Rubens found his brother Philip again in Rome. He was librarian to Cardinal Ascanio Colonna, and was thus able to smooth Rubens' path into the highest Roman society, and to bring him in contact with men of consequence in the Church. He spent little time among artists, whom he found too Bohemian—later, in a letter to the German physician Johann Faber about the premature death of his compatriot, the painter Elsheimer, he was to deplore the deceased's 'sin of sloth'. Instead he preferred to move among archaeologists. Taking their advice, he multiplied his studies and sketches from the antique. Some of these came into Philip's hands, and he published five of

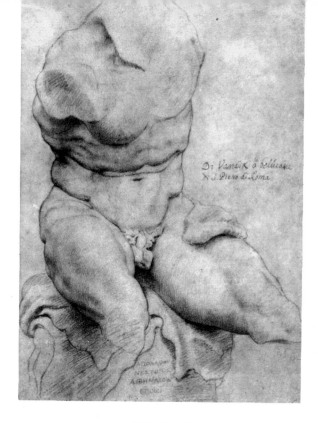

24　*Belvedere Torso*

them in a work which appeared in Antwerp in 1608, under the
imprint of Moretus, successor to the famous Plantin, bearing the
title *Electorum Libri duo*. They were engraved by Corneille Galle.

These researches must have fascinated Rubens the humanist. They
formed a basis of solid learning which was drawn on not only in
his later paintings but in his relations with scholars and princes.
His life would have been a most agreeable one had not money worries
continued to harass him; it was, as he said, 'from pure necessity'
that he consented to undertake any other work than that demanded
by his studies. This did not prevent him from supplementing his
resources in a way which brought credit to himself and the Duke.
He made a point of this when the Duke was insisting on his return

to Mantua: could he, 'without deserving a thousand censures, abandon this commission so gloriously won from the greatest masters of Rome'?[21] The altarpiece which the Oratorian Fathers had ordered from him, thanks perhaps to Cardinal Borghese's intervention in the final stages of a determined competition among several painters, was his first important commission, and it was in order to bring it to a satisfactory conclusion that Rubens was asking Vincenzo Gonzaga to allow him to prolong his stay in Rome.

As soon as it was finished, the *Adoration of the Virgin by Angels and Saints* won universal admiration; but it could not be mounted in the intended place because it caught the light in an unfortunate way. 'One can hardly distinguish the figures,' wrote Rubens, most upset, to Chieppio[25], 'or enjoy the perfection of the colours, the style of the faces and the folds of the draperies, though they have been treated with extreme care, and are done from nature; and are agreed by everyone to be beautiful!'

He was obliged, therefore, to paint a second version, this time on slate, a material which absorbs oil and prevents a shiny finish. This painting is divided into three sections: a central panel, with two lateral pieces. In comparing this second version, still in the Church of Sta Maria in Valicella, with the first, which is at the Grenoble Museum, the question arises whether the matter of lighting—a real enough difficulty, as a visit to the church will show—was really the only reason for the Oratorian Fathers' objections. The fashion of Caravaggio's style and technique, with its robust figures, powerful masses, and strong contrasts between light and shade, was gaining influence. The Fathers, incited probably by the artists whom Rubens had supplanted, did not wish to lag behind other churches. As for Rubens, he did not wish to offend the Romans—least of all the wealthy Oratorians. He agreed, therefore, in spite of his own feelings, to bow to their wishes, and repainted the picture as ordered. The saints of the lateral sections are deliberately inspired by antique statues, and the contrasts of lighting are no less striking than those of the illustrious Michelangelo Merisi himself, surnamed Caravaggio, who had, after being the terror of the Church, become its greatest painter.

The central portion has, in spite of its conventional look, hints of brightness and golden tints so suggestive of Rubens' manner that one imagines the conflict between the painter's own taste and the fashion which inhibited him. The whole, however, remains dull and without warmth; it has neither the ease nor freshness nor the decorative scale of the Grenoble painting, whose best qualities continued to assert themselves under Rubens' brush. The figures, conceived on the grand scale, full and vigorous, stand firmly on the ground; the architecture, of a classical nobility, is enlivened by the flight of angels round the Madonna; and the lighting, very happily contrived, bathes the whole scene in an atmosphere of tenderness which is at once subtle and brilliant. The movement of the whole is one of controlled expressionism, in which the painter moderates the emphasis he gives to his figures by their profound vitality, and places their pure spirituality at the service of an intense and vital dynamism.

The *Adoration of the Shepherds* in the Church of S. Filippo Neri at Fermo, which was painted at the same period as the pictures in the Church of Sta Maria in Valicella, shows how much trouble Rubens was prepared to take to avoid offence and conform to fashionable aesthetics. This painting was also commissioned by the Oratorians, and Rubens did not wish to meet with the same difficulties he had had in Rome.

At first glance, the painting is disappointing with its dull colouring and the hardness of its expression. The bright tones seem buried under an accumulation of dead browns, and all the weight of the authority of Ludwig Burchard and Roberto Longhi, who discovered this work, was needed for its attribution to Rubens to gain acceptance[26]. None of the virtues displayed by the artist are to be seen.

Unbeknown to Rubens, this was the end of his stay in Rome. At this age, approaching thirty, he appears to have been a skilful artist, strong in both observation and understanding, drawing by turns on the masters of his choice and the schools which nourished his talents, and blending adroitly and masterfully, in search of his own style, all fashions and influences. 'Italianizing' and personal by turns, on the one hand he manipulated formulas, made concessions to the tastes of his clients and was inclined rather to be carried along by the stream than to swim against it. On the other hand, he sought continually to establish on firm foundations his own language: broad, spacious, robust, and alive, as the paintings of the old Flemish school, with their sober and powerful realism, were alive. Thus Rubens, the masterly orchestrator, the prodigious harmonist, slowly but surely drew closer to the style in which he was to fulfil himself when, having at last succeeded in reconciling the demands of his vision with the expression of his own time and place, he would produce his epic.

For the moment, he was very much put out by having his rejected picture on his hands. Then he conceived the idea of persuading the Duke of Mantua to buy it. First, in order to obtain some money; and then, because he considered, as he told Chieppio, that 'it would not be to my honour to leave in Rome two similar paintings from my hand'.

So the courtier selected his finest quill and suggested to his employer, through the inevitable Chieppio, the purchase of the work in question. It should have cost Vincenzo 800 crowns, but Rubens agreed to a considerable reduction. He left it to the 'discretion of your Most Serene Highness, to which I leave also whatever terms of payment your Highness wishes'.[27] He knew by experience the complications of the Duke's treasury; but he also knew how bad a payer he was. Hence his precaution, skilfully presented as a simple request for an advance: 'I shall content myself with asking him for the hundred or two hundred crowns on account, which I need to carry out my copying.'[28] In the meantime the picture remained in the church, covered up.

Unfortunately Vincenzo Gonzaga was not convinced. Rubens, infuriated, was up in arms. Offhand and haughty by turns, he wrote to Chieppio that the Duke had done well not to accept his offer, since he was no longer in such a hurry to sell the picture. He added that since it had been 'exhibited for several days in the same church, in excellent conditions of lighting, it has been seen and greatly applauded by the whole city!' So much so, in fact, that 'I am now certain of finding a purchaser for it here in Rome.'[29]

Modest enough when his position demanded it, but crushing, disdainful, even arrogant when he had nothing to fear and was sure of himself, Rubens now treated the Duke of Mantua in a high-handed fashion. His own situation in Rome was excellent; he was on good terms with many people, and he had plenty of commissions. What had he henceforth to do with this princeling, this playboy, this plotter, who in spite of his extravagance was without fortune, and who lacked even the power to send Rubens to Paris to paint pictures of pretty women? He had made a firm decision to stay in Rome and pursue his career in spite of the protests of Vincenzo Gonzaga when, at the end of October 1608, he received disturbing news about his mother's health. He at once informed the Duke, through Chieppio, of his sudden departure—'insane haste pursues me'—and set out without even passing through Mantua, adding hypocritically: 'On my return I say no more than that I shall obey every wish of my Most Serene patron, conforming to his will as to an inviolable law, in all places, at all times... Coming back, then, from Flanders, I shall proceed directly to Mantua. This will afford me pleasure for many reasons; particularly that of being able to be of service by my presence to your Highness.'[30]

Maria Pypelinckx died on 15 November, some weeks before Rubens arrived there in mid-December. She was seventy-two. Two of her children had predeceased her; two others, Philip and Peter Paul, had been far away from her. She died alone and courageously, taking with her to the grave a secret which preyed on her.

The painter, who was unable to get rid of his rejected picture and had to take it to Flanders with him, had it placed two years later, in 1610, near his mother's tomb behind the altar of the Holy Sacrament in the minster-abbey of St-Michel, where it remained until the French invasion of Belgium. Taken to France, it was presented by the state to the Grenoble Museum in 1811.

Rubens was now thirty-one. As he had done before, he strolled about the port of Antwerp with his eyes fixed in space; but the people, knowing of his successes in Italy, looked on him with curiosity and greeted him even with respect. Women found his lordliness, his lively eyes and his elegance attractive; as for the painters, they mistrusted so much self-assurance in a colleague. Perhaps he had brought back from beyond the Alps something which would revolutionize Flemish painting, vegetating as it was on the banks of the Scheldt among its formulas, its influences and its borrowings? Rubens was indeed preparing to throw into the mould of Flanders the bullion and spoils of his Italian campaign.

CHAPTER FOUR

Peace or turmoil

The people of Antwerp regarded the life led by their Archduke and his wife with something approaching amazement. Their court, in the image of the Spanish court, was not simply that of prince and princess—of a pretty, kind-hearted Isabella and an austere, retiring and rather ill-favoured Albert—but that of God himself. Everything was subordinated to its veneration. The city of speculation, negotiation, shady dealing and easy virtue, had become a community of penitents and bigots. The women wore homespun and spent most of their time at church services; the men scourged themselves in public during processions. This was not Spain but a caricature of Spain. Its atmosphere was one of fear: the Flemish feared, deep down, that they might attain to a more or less desired Heaven at the cost of their own souls.

The seventeen provinces were divided into two unalterably opposed groups: the Calvinist North and the Catholic South. From the pallet on which he lay dying in terrible suffering, his body 'stinking, pierced with nails and covered with lice', his eyes turned towards the window where he could see the priest who officiated for him at the high altar of the Escorial, Philip II contemplated this distant land, victim of the worst kind of war: that which sets father against son and husband against wife. Unity, which might have been possible a few years earlier, was no longer so: the Dutch, having established their government and ensured their commercial freedom, were content with their lot. Only hypocrisy, calculation or pure illusion could claim that the Spanish King's granting of the appearance of independence to the Catholic Low Countries would lead one day to the reconciliation of all dissidents. This had been done by means of the Act of Cession of 6 May 1598, which created his daughter the Infanta Isabella (who was to marry the Archduke Albert a few months later) Regent of the Netherlands. But there remained the clauses of the treaty which deprived the Flemings of their liberty, for example by forbidding all commerce with Spanish possessions in America on pain of confiscation of goods and even death; and the secret clauses which subjected the government of the Low Countries in all its aspects to orders from Madrid, imposed the presence of Spanish garrisons in Antwerp, Ghent, Cambrai and two or three other strategic places, enjoined the pursuit of heretics until their conversion, and finally implied the prosecution of the war against Holland until such time as that country returned to the bosom of Catholic Spain. However, Philip II died on 13 September 1598.

The Archduke and Isabella reigned, but they hardly governed. At the most, their piety, intelligence and reasonableness made it appear that the period of fear and violence was over. But however repugnant it was to them as lovers of peace, the war must be continued. Albert having little talent for strategy, the state junta, which feared his pacifism more than it did his military ineptitude, decided to remove him from the command of the Spanish army of occupation and give it to a highranking officer who was to come from Madrid. Isabella, affronted, made protests, but Albert recovered himself and decided that if they wanted a professional soldier as generalissimo, he would choose one himself. He chose a Genoese, Ambrogio Spinola. The King and his ministers refused. Never should it be said that the 'tercios' were under the orders of a foreign mercenary! Finally, as the Regents held firm, their nomination was accepted. Philip III bowed, but would not send a peseta to his brother-in-law, who had in consequence to make incessant demands for the wherewithal to feed and equip the army. A few highly-trained regiments would have been quite sufficient to finish with the rebels, but faced with the inertia of Madrid the war had to be conducted as efficiently as possible with the resources available. Above all, peace must be sought.

The Regents could achieve nothing more than the truce of 1609. For twelve years the nightmare was over. It was now necessary to demonstrate that the government was not just a Spanish puppet government, and that it wished for a return to confidence and prosperity. This was an immense task, overshadowed as it was by the bloody memories of Alba's massacres, of pillage and auto-da-fé. After the golden age of the previous century, Flanders now experienced an economic stagnation which appeared insoluble so long as the people of Holland kept the Scheldt closed to trade. It was to this atmosphere of uncertainty and bitterness that Rubens returned after his eight years' absence.

He was not, as some people have thought, welcomed like the Prodigal Son; on the other hand he was regarded with curiosity, interest, and even deference. Even before his departure for Italy, his artistic production had been that of a recognized talent and a powerful personality. The Flemish are not subject to unreasoning enthusiasm; they see things as they are, without passion or exaggeration. It was true that the son of the exiled magistrate had had many commissions in Italy, but his reputation had not gone beyond a fairly small circle; and even if he had painted huge compositions for certain churches in Rome, there was no doubt that the Archduke's protection and the introductions secured for him by his brother had played their part. Apart from that, he would hardly attract the attention of connoisseurs simply because of his position with the Duke of Mantua, who was, after all, only a princeling without much real power or prestige.

Still, he was Rubens. That is to say that in his own eyes he had a name and works to live up to. His letters[31] show his character, though we should realize that they show only the less intimate side of it. The surviving correspondence reveals for the most part the courtier, the diplomat, the politician and the man of business. His family letters were lost in a fire at the Comte de Bergeyck's house in Brussels in 1702 or 1703; Bergeyck was heir to the second husband of Hélène Fourment, the painter's widow.

Rubens' name and works were at this time small compared with his ambitions; they were considerable, however, compared with what other Flemish painters had done in Italy or brought back from there. And we know only fragments of his total production. Personally, the impression he gave was brilliant: he was eloquent, charming, enlightening, convincing. Though he was a zealous courtier, he had been capable of telling Vincenzo Gonzaga what he thought of the sinister Chieppio, and of refusing point-blank when the Duke had wanted him to go and paint pretty ladies' portraits in Paris. Because he had an elevated idea of his art, Rubens spoke of it nobly; and if he allowed people to make use of him as a man, he demanded that they respect him as a painter. His reply to the order given him at Valladolid to restore the paintings damaged by rain is significant: 'It is my principle never to allow myself to be mistaken for another man, however great a man he may be.' And the twenty-six-year-old painter was not afraid to add: 'I should harm my reputation, which is not unknown in Spain, were I to sign work which was mediocre and unworthy of me.'

He was a man of some piety. If his character was not austere, at least he had no love of ostentation. He preferred to choose his friends from learned circles rather than from the society of presumptuous, extravagant and vainglorious princes. This was the man who moved into the family residence in the Place du Meir where his mother had died. The solid citizen was also an indefatigable worker. Nothing was more important than his work, and he executed it with all the punctuality and seriousness which he gave to political and diplomatic business. Throughout his activities—even in his love affairs—he showed great self-control; he was never carried away, despite his taste for the generous charms of his charming compatriots. His work was an outlet, it is true, for his excessive sensuality; but in any case he never concealed it, being without hypocrisy in any sphere. Well-balanced in all senses of the word, Rubens would one day have inscribed on the façade of the pavilion in his garden his Rule of Life, in the form of two triplets from Juvenal to this effect:

'Let us leave to the gods the care of dispensing their benefits to us and of giving us what we most need. They love men better than men love themselves.'

'Let us ask them only for health of body and soundness of mind, for a strong soul free from the fear of death and untouched by anger or by vain desires.'

The Stoic philosophy of this inscription reflects the humanist temperament of a man whose faith was deep, confident and exempt from doubts. Every morning before starting work he would hear mass, for this master of pagan ceremonies was also the painter of the Counter-Reformation and of the Church Triumphant. And did not man owe his pleasures as well as his sufferings to the Creator?

Antwerp was not Mantua or Rome. Its people were more serious, diligent and laborious than the Latins whose enthusiasms and fickleness—and even whose changes and contradictions of character— he had experienced. For although he had produced much in Italy, he had also had his troubles, and these had been due less to his own failings than to those of his employers; nor was he in a hurry to forget the vexations to which he had been put by the Oratorians' refusal of his picture.

Philip, who was three years his elder, also lived in the house in the Place du Meir. The *Electorum Libri Duo* which he published with Moretus, with Peter Paul's drawings, is dated 1608, and we know that the engraver Corneille Galle's work was finished before 8 August of this year. The illustrations had therefore been sent to Antwerp from Italy, since Rubens had not known that his return would be so sudden. His brother probably reached Antwerp at the

25 *Adoration of the Magi.* Detail of pl. 30

same time, and the two of them found the work completed in the printer's workshop. So that it was as the author of these archaeological drawings that the painter returned to Antwerp. One may imagine that he was not altogether pleased about this, since he was liable to be taken for an 'antiquarian,' even for a 'Romanist', while in fact he had deliberately turned towards the future. Indeed he had proved this by his interest in Baroque painting in Italy, and by taking his inspiration in the two commissions he fulfilled before his departure—those of Sta Maria in Valicella in Rome and S. Filippo Neri at Fermo—from the style of Caravaggio then in fashion.

This slightly ambiguous situation caused the painter to display, during the first few months of his return to Antwerp, a certain irresolution. What was his true course? Towards Italianism or towards realism of a specifically Flemish kind? His first commissions would give the answer.

The Archduke Albert sent for Rubens from Brussels where he resided. He had asked Vincenzo Gonzaga, seven years earlier, to allow his court painter to go to Rome to carry out for him the paintings intended for the Church of Santa Croce in Gerusalemme. He was aware of Rubens' merit and of his talent, and thought with good reason that his stay in Italy could only have developed his capabilities. At the same time Rubens attracted the attention of Nicolas Rockox, a magistrate like his own father, and several times Burgomaster-in-Chief of the city. His first patrons after his return were, therefore, two men of considerable importance: the Governor of Flanders himself, and one of the foremost personages in Antwerp. This extraordinary position of honour tempts one to search for hidden explanations, but such a search is vain: the simple fact is that very few painters have ever enjoyed the favour which Rubens did at that age.

In 1609 the deputy-mayors of Antwerp, impelled by the 'buitenburgmester' Nicolas Rockox, decided to finish the decoration of the Statenkamer, or room of state, in the Town Hall. They adorned it with a bronze crucifix by Giambologna bought from Jan Brueghel I, and commissioned Abraham Janssens to symbolize *The Genius of Antwerp and the Scheldt*. Anton de Succa was to paint portraits of former sovereigns. Rubens was given the task of completing these decorations with an *Adoration of the Magi*. Two years later Nicolas Rockox was again the originator of an important Antwerp commission for the painter: the *Descent from the Cross* for the Chapel of the Serment des Arquebusiers in the Cathedral of Notre-Dame.

Nine months after his return, on 23 September 1609, Rubens was appointed 'painter to the palace of their Serene Highnesses' at an annual salary of 500 francs. Would he move to Brussels to live the life of the scintillating court? Antwerp held him. He himself knew very well how to choose between this wounded city to which he owed so much of his new prosperity, and the worldly glories of the capital. The Archduke Albert understood his reasons for this decision and gave him his permission to stay in the city of his choice.

Less than two weeks after this flattering appointment Rubens married, on 3 October, at the Church of St-Michel, where his mother lay buried, a girl called Isabella Brandt, fourteen years his junior. In order to live comfortably, to receive clients and friends, and to be able to work at his ease, he purchased, two-and-a-half years later, on 4 January 1610, a respectable dwelling which today forms part of the 'Maison de Rubens'. Of his union with the attractive Isabella, who was the daughter of a scholarly humanist, Clerk of the Court of the City of Antwerp, and thus, as Jan Rubens had been, linked to the municipality, three children were born: Clara-Serena, baptized on 21 March 1611, who died at the age of twelve; Albert, baptized on 5 June 1614, who later succeeded his father as Secretary to the Privy Council; and finally Nicolas, baptized on 23 March 1618. These two died in 1657 and 1655 respectively.

Rubens was now faced with the first of his works which would adorn a public place in the city in which he had chosen to live. It did not take him a year to finish it: on 29 April 1610 the *Adoration of the Magi* was already in place in the Statenkamer of the Town Hall. It was not to remain there long; two years later it was presented to Don Rodrigo Calderón, Count of Oliva, the King of Spain's ambassador, who took it to Madrid. In 1621, when Oliva's goods were confiscated, the painting passed to Philip IV, who had it enlarged by Rubens himself during his visit to the Spanish capital in 1628. The painter added angels above the picture, and to the right a procession of Magi, animals and horsemen among whom he himself is represented. This addition destroyed the unity of this lively

26   *Portrait of a young Girl*

composition. The sketch belonging to the Gemeente-Museum of Groningen, with its vibrant colouring, is more expressive than the fine but disfigured picture now in the Prado.

About ten years after the Antwerp *Adoration of the Magi*, Rubens carried out a large composition on the same theme which the Royal Museum of Brussels acquired from the Church of the Capuchins at Tournai; then in 1619 the painting at St-Jean-de-Malines; then the one executed for the Abbey of St-Michel in 1624, which is now in the Antwerp Museum *(Pl. 28)*, and finally, in 1634, the *Ador-ation of the Magi* of the Chapelle des Dames Blanches in Louvain which is now at King's College, Cambridge. He made further versions of the famous New Testament scene, but the greatest of them remains the magnificent painting in the Antwerp Museum.

Rubens had now chosen his course. The elaborate emphasis of the Italians was mitigated by an acute sense of realism: the crowded figures in the procession of the kings are presented as an astonishing play of living forms, whose shapes and movement are dictated by the Rubens style. This style was born in Rome. It owes much of its scale to Michelangelo and to Caravaggio, but it is the blending of many types of figures closely studied and observed. Its dimensions are developed to such an extent that on occasion it becomes extra-vagant, affected, or inflated. But with Rubens this eloquence does not seem superimposed. Rather it is an overflowing of vitality, an exaltation of the ardour of life; and when it joins with Baroque expressionism, the result is the conquering style which Rubens makes into a kind of dynamic movement.

Without being directly inspired by the technique of Caravaggio which Rubens had absorbed in Rome, the *Adoration of the Magi* in the Prado contains strong contrasts of light and shade without, however, suggesting any deliberate seeking for effect. The daylight of the foreground and the glow of the torches brandished by the figures in the middle ground create by their contrast with the darker portions of the picture a liveliness which is emphasized by the broad rhythm of masses.

The composition, in the form of an oblique arrow terminating in the king kneeling at the feet of the Christ child held by the Virgin, the king being accompanied by a beautiful fair-haired page, is classic. On the right Rubens has painted the vigorous nude figures of work-ers from the Antwerp docks, here bringing presents to the divine infant. Italian influence is evident in the play of muscles and the tension of sinews.

27   *The Holy Trinity*, 1620

The Virgin is of the type which corresponds to Rubens' ideal as portrayed in *The Virgin adored by Angels and Saints* in Grenoble, and its double in Sta Maria in Valicella. This attractive woman, pleasantly seductive, whose flesh becomes so important in the nudity of later profane paintings, has nonetheless a completely virginal modesty; her face and gestures breathe her innocence and radiate grace. Little by little Rubens' two wives were to be substituted for this type, which can be regarded as the epitome of the artist's first choice of love partner undergoing transformation by his creative power.

In the *Adoration of the Magi* the painter asserted the dramatic power and turbulence of forms which he was to develop in so many huge ecclesiastical paintings. He was now past thirty and, through nine years spent in measuring his own powers and studying his masters, had won his creative freedom. He was to develop this freedom with astonishing facility; and the calm regularity with which he would produce one canvas after another came to have something majestic about it, like the movement of an ocean. He was a complete stranger to the idea of regrets or second thoughts; even when he painted the same subject several times he would re-create it as if he had never attempted it before.

He was hopelessly in love with Isabella and did not hide it. With him, in any case, everything happened as it were in broad daylight; he was even anxious that Antwerp should witness his happiness. In *Rubens and Isabella Brandt (Pl. 33)*, he abandons turbulence for serenity, Italian exuberance for the bourgeois realism of Flanders. Isabella, posing sweetly for posterity, has tenderly placed her hand upon him. The charming young couple in their finery look out at us from a bower touched with autumn tints. He is on a bench, and she sits at his feet—which unbalances the composition a little. Both are happy and confident. Pretty Isabella smiles, half shyly, half mischievously; Rubens' left hand rests on the pommel of his sword (had he a right to this aristocratic weapon?) as if to protect her.

74

28 *Adoration of the Magi*, 1624

29   *Portrait of a Man*

30   *Brazen Serpent, c.* 1619

The colouring is surprising in its dullness which is at odds with
the happy atmosphere of the picture. The severity of Flemish realism
dominates the picture, whose sincerity might have called for a luminosity more in keeping with the subject. But the painter probably
wished to show that what he had learnt in Italy had not caused him
to forget his origins. It is no coincidence that this painting should
have been carried out at a time when, as well as marrying a young
Flemish woman, he had moved to the centre of Antwerp and taken
up his post as painter to the Archduke and his wife. His marriage
indeed was to a place as well as to a person.

He worked without interruption and his studio was crowded with
paintings. Receiving orders from every quarter, he was obliged to
obtain assistants. When the Brussels engraver Jacques de Bie recom-

31   *Portrait of Archduke Albert, c.* 1635

mended a young man to him, he replied on 11 May 1611: 'I am so besieged[32] that there are apprentices who have been waiting for years, under other masters, for me to be able to accept them.' He added that he had been obliged 'truly, and without exaggeration... to turn away more than a hundred aspirants', among whom were young men of his own family and those of his best friends.

Before Rubens had completed the *Adoration of the Magi* he was working on other orders, including several portraits.   As court

32 *Portrait of the Infanta Isabella, c. 1635*

painter he was, traditionally, expected to paint for the courts of
Europe portraits of his sovereigns Albert and Isabella. This task
he returned to at intervals for several years: for example, in 1625
he undertook a further series of portraits of the Archduchess on the
occasion of the taking of Breda. These large numbers of portraits,
which may be seen at the National Gallery in London, at the Kunsthistorisches Museum in Vienna, at the Pinakothek in Lugano, and
elsewhere, are simply cold and official tasks: part of the duties which

Rubens carried out with a good grace, in the knowledge that this work would some day represent the price of his freedom.

To fulfil orders he painted every kind of picture—portraits, genre paintings, mythical and religious subjects—turning them out in large quantities. One work painted during 1609-10 is particularly striking. It is the model, belonging to the Louvre, for a large painting in the Prado: *Philopoemen, General of the Acheans, recognized by an old Woman (Pl. 36)*. This was for a long time attributed to Adriaen van Utrecht. Several Spanish catalogues mention it as being the work of Rubens and Snyders. But the masterly style of the former is easily recognizable.

This panel illustrates an anecdote about the recognition of Philopoemen, who is dressed as a peasant, by an old woman, from the way he splits wood. She and her husband are restraining the famous warrior from carrying on his menial task. The main interest of the painting, however, is in the magnificent still-life in the foreground which occupies three-quarters of the picture. In it can be found all the joyous Baroque style, the virtuosity and sureness in handling paint, the glow and the richness of the great painter of Antwerp —the only man who could at that period have produced such a work.

Rubens was at this time contemplating a studio to fulfil his numerous orders, where he would be master, surrounded not only by his apprentices and pupils, but also already known painters who would study with him. Even if the theory that the Philopoemen still-life was painted as a model for Snyders seems doubtful, this sumptuous collection of game must nevertheless have been, for the artist, one of those 'pieces of bravura' likely to encourage and inspire his collaborators. It seems reasonable to suppose that Rubens wished to spread the Baroque 'grand manner' among the Antwerp artists working with him.

The *Annunciation* in the Kunsthistorisches Museum, and the sketch *Samson and Delilah* in the Chicago Art Institute, whose main elements are repeated in a painting of three or four years later, can both be ascribed to 1609-10. So can the *Brazen Serpent* in Sir Francis Cook's collection, which is typical of the beginning of Rubens' Antwerp period.

This was also the period of two major works carried out for the Church of St Paul. In Jacques de Wit's description of the churches of Antwerp, which dates from the eighteenth century, he attributes to Rubens the *Adoration of the Shepherds* in the Church of St Paul, where there was also the *Glorification of the Holy Sacrament by the Church Fathers*, which was engraved in 1643 by Snyders, with Rubens' name. The attribution of the St Paul *Adoration* has often been questioned; but this canvas, though larger, is very similar to the painting of the same subject done for the Church of S. Filippo Neri in Fermo in 1608, and when the Antwerp painting was removed and cleaned during the Second World War, the similarities of style between the two became unmistakable. The St Paul canvas of which a sketch exists in the Hermitage, is much freer in style than the Fermo version, which aimed at pleasing the Italian admirers of Caravaggio. In the Antwerp painting one can imagine the relief of the artist at being free to express himself without reference to models. The colouring is more harmonious, the paint applied with greater fluidity. M. van Puyvelde even sees in it 'Van Gogh before his time'. However that may be, a comparison between the three works—the sketch and the two paintings—spaced out over the course of a year, is relevant to Rubens' development from his sojourn in Italy to the beginnings of his Antwerp period.

The *Glorification of the Holy Sacrament* although inspired by the famous *Disputà* has neither the scale, the knowledge, nor the liveliness of the Raphael composition in the Vatican. It is certainly by Rubens, since an inventory of 1616 certifies its presence in one of the chapels of the Church of St Paul at that time. But this unbalanced, cramped composition has none of the qualities of power and concentration —or the subtlety in execution—of other paintings of the same period. The colouring, which is dull and without accent, is another reason

33 *Rubens and Isabella Brandt in the Honeysuckle Bower,* 1609

34 Inner courtyard of Rubens'
house in Antwerp

35 Rubens' house
and garden in Antwerp

for supposing that the artist may have painted this in a perfunctory
manner. Rubens' style, which is such a personal one, has disappeared,
leaving only an insipid systematization. At the same time Rubens
cannot be blamed for the enlarging of the picture in 1656 to fit
the new altar—a regrettable operation.

The wrong, however, was soon to be righted: about June 1610
the triptych *Raising of the Cross* was ordered to be painted for the
high altar of the Church of St Walburge by the Church Council
members and the patron and collector, Cornelius van der Geest.
Rubens began working on it at the house of his father-in-law Jan
Brandt, where he stayed before buying and moving into his own
house. He finished it in the church itself, so that it would fit into
its surroundings. A canvas screen built by dock workers protected

36 *Philopoemen, General of the Acheans, recognized by an old Woman,*
c. 1618

it from the eyes of the curious. The *Raising of the Cross*—a theme
already treated by Rubens in 1602 in Rome—adorned the high
altar of St Walburge until 1794, when it was removed to Paris.
Restored to Antwerp in 1815, it was placed in the Cathedral, where
it is today, as St Walburge was pulled down in 1798 to make room
for harbour improvements.

CHAPTER FIVE

Extending the horizon

From the time of his arrival in Antwerp and his marriage, Rubens wished for his own house. He acquired a respectable one in the residential district of Wapper, in the Vaarstraat (canal street). He paid its owner, Dr Andreas Backaert, 7,600 florins, and immediately began to think of ways to enlarge and arrange it to his own taste —that of a successful man who liked comfort, space, light, and beautiful objects. Having a large and important circle of acquaintances, he had to be able to entertain—and not only his fellow-citizens but also foreign noblemen whom he had met on his travels or missions abroad. He also had to be able to receive his Archduke and Archduchess, and his important admirers. And the size of the paintings they ordered needed correspondingly large spaces. Rubens was not fond of working, as he had done for the *Raising of the Cross*, on the site, and in discomfort.

People have often spoken of Rubens' 'palace'. The term is, however, unjustified. The house was neither ostentatious nor luxurious; it was the house of a comfortable citizen rather than a prince or a parvenu. Unfortunately recent additions have given it an appearance of sumptuousness which belies its real nature: it was the setting of a laborious life completely devoted to art.

Rubens purchased a plot adjacent to this house and built on it a studio 40 by 26 feet; two of its façades were adorned with statues and high reliefs *(Pl. 37)*. Little by little, as his fame and wealth increased, he extended the property, building (presumably to his own design) a portico with three bays to connect the studio to the house, and a pavilion at the bottom of the garden to rest in. The

37   School of Van Dyck, *The Studio of Rubens*

portico is decorated in the heavy Baroque style reflecting contemporary taste; the Italianate exterior of the whole is majestic, whereas the interior is more modest and 'bourgeois'. 'Between the courtyard and garden,' writes Roger de Piles, 'he built a circular room, like the Pantheon in Rome, lit only from a single opening above. This room is full of busts, antique statues and valuable paintings brought back from Italy, together with other rare and interesting objects.' The size of his collection forced Rubens to distribute it throughout the house: 'In the past year I have spent several thousand florins ornamenting my house,' he wrote on 12 May to Sir Dudley Carleton, the British Ambassador to the United Provinces at The Hague, with whom he had various transactions involving works of art.

Rubens' house was for the most part preserved in its original condition until the eighteenth century. After that, successive owners

38 *Old Woman warming herself*, 1622

39   *The Four Philosophers, c.* 1615

made various alterations. When, in 1937, it became the property
of the city of Antwerp it was carefully restored to the condition in
which Rubens had left it at his death.

He spent most of his time here. His nephew Philip reported to
Roger de Piles how Rubens' day was divided. The artist rose at
four, heard mass, and then worked until five in the afternoon when,
in order to relax from his fatigues and worries he went riding 'or
did something else to refresh his mind'. He dined frugally, having

'a strong aversion to excessive drinking and luxurious eating, as well as to gaming. His greatest pleasures were to ride a fine Spanish horse, to read a book, and to study the medals, agates, cornelians and other intaglios, of which he possessed a very fine collection...'[33] Thus he worked at least twelve hours a day; when he was at work he always had, 'at his side, a reader employed to read aloud from some good book: usually Plutarch, Livy or Seneca.'[34] Though Philip Rubens need not be taken literally, what he says—he was 29 when the painter died—is probably an accurate reflection of a life which we know was largely devoted to working. Rubens' nephew is anxious to shine himself, as well as to add to the fame of his family (which was unnecessary); and it is difficult to accept as the exact

40　*Raising of the Cross*

truth all the information he passed on to de Piles for his *Vita Petri Pauli Rubenii*.   De Piles was a connoisseur and a theoretician, a typical seventeenth-century 'inquirer'—more a compiler than a witness—whose uncritical acceptance of such material sometimes leads one to suspect his conclusions; they must always be closely examined.

At this point one may note Rubens' taste for physics and astronomy, and his interest in the first experiments with the microscope.   He corresponded regularly not only with politicians and diplomats, but with scholars like the humanist Peiresc, to whom he wrote at least once a week for seventeen years, and who much appreciated his letters.   Together with Justus Lipsius, whose portrait appears in a painting by Rubens, *The Four Philosophers*[35], of 1614 or 1615 *(Pl. 39)*, the painter is a perfect representative of Flemish Christian humanism.   His library was rich in philosophical and scientific works.

The *Raising of the Cross* was placed in the Church of St Walburge, where crowds came to admire it.   Fromentin said later that this work, together with the *Descent from the Cross*, ordered the following year, constituted Rubens' 'first act as the leader of a school'.   From this point the destinies of Antwerp and Rubens, admirer and embellisher, were closely connected.

The learned men of the Counter-Reformation, anxious to substitute truth—or at least veracity—for tradition, were at pains to decide whether Christ had been nailed to the Cross already erected, or while it was lying on the ground.   The Jesuits, who organized the new iconography, disagreed among themselves on this point; but since the artists were unanimous in representing Christ nailed to a Cross lying on the ground and then raised by human hands, they accepted this interpretation, which spread among their churches.   On the now demolished ceiling of St-Charles-Borromée, the church of the Order in Antwerp, Rubens painted a Christ lying on the Cross and being lifted up by the executioners—the sketch is in the Louvre *(Pl. 40)*—which was inspired by the masterpiece in the Cathedral.

He thus contributed to the spreading of this tragic theme throughout Flanders and France.

He presented this work to the Archduke's delegate, the clergy, the churchwardens, to Cornelius van der Geest, the aristocracy and the whole population of the town whose reigning artist he was. Never had such passionate lyricism been seen under a church roof. The convulsed movement of the bodies, the atmosphere of horror and fear in which the divine victim, at the mercy of fury and hate, is surrounded with an unearthly radiance above the tangled mass of executioners bracing their legs or hauling on ropes, were beyond anything that had been seen before. Biceps and pectoral muscles stand out; grunts of exertion are forced from open mouths; features are distorted by the effort of raising the heavy Cross; and the tempest bows and shakes the trees. Physical tumult on this scale expresses with terrible intensity the pain and suffering and injustice associated with this subject.

There are certain reminders in this work of the *Raising of the Cross* painted in Rome; but here the daring of the diagonal composition is underlined by the violence of the treatment. The brush appears to assault the canvas with a kind of fury. The impasto is heavy. The plastic strength of this painting may well derive from Michelangelo, from Caravaggio, and even from the Bolognese painters; but the colouring is beyond their influence. More alive and brilliant, it follows the movement of the composition by means of suggestive touches rather than contrast. It is in this way that Rubens detaches the strongly-lit figure of Christ from the browns and greys which surround Him.

In the right-hand panel a centurion on a rearing horse turns back towards the soldiers dragging one of the thieves to his cross; the other thief is stretched out on the ground, ready to be bound to his. In the left-hand panel Mary and St John the Apostle are standing; she is resigned and silent. She looks with infinite sadness at her son, and St John places his hand consolingly on hers. At their feet, and contrasting with their dignity, the holy women sobbing, wringing their hands or throwing themselves back and hugging their terrified infants, form a concentrated patch of emotion. On the reverse side of the left-hand panel, St Eligius and St Walburge are depicted; on that of the right-hand panel, St Catherine and St Amand.

The dynamism and power of this canvas suggest that Rubens had broken away from the Italian influence for good. At this period he was still in the habit of making a large number of studies before beginning on a painting. Those that survive for the *Raising of the Cross* include the studies for the body of Christ (Weisbach collection, Berlin; Grenville Lindall Winthrop collection, New York); that for the naked executioner supporting the Cross (Ashmolean Museum, Oxford); and the hands of the Virgin (Albertina, Vienna). Dulwich College owns the sketch for the exterior of the panels.

One wonders how much surprise was felt by the Flemings. Admittedly their Italianate painters had accustomed them to large and vigorous forms; but no one had gone so far as this in tragic eloquence, in expression and movement. No one had dared put such muscular realism into religious painting. The foot and calf of St Michael, placed gratuitously in the foreground of Caravaggio's picture in the Church of San Luigi dei Francesi in Rome had aroused the unconcealed consternation of the Canons. In the *Raising of the Cross* it was not the thighs of the executioners or the naked breast of the woman in the left-hand panel which shocked (this sort of thing had been seen in other paintings): it was the fact that Rubens had dared attack the conformism of Flemish painters which insisted on moderation in religious painting. The daring he exhibited in throwing the composition off balance, where his compatriots would have carefully weighed and divided their masses and planes; his vigorous execution as compared with their smoothness: these were revolutionary. The *Raising of the Cross* was accepted, but Rubens saw that he had in fact gone too far. Possibly he was told so by someone in authority. At any rate he had no sooner found his own style than he was obliged to abandon it. The academic and theatrical *Descent from the Cross*, begun in 1611, has nothing in common with the epic and lyrical *Raising*.

For the son of the exiled magistrate to succeed in Antwerp, favoured by princes and collectors, to receive orders from the city, the church and the archducal palace, and to live securely and comfortably, it was necessary to have all the most powerful people on his side and to pay attention to their opinions. They were inclined to reprove his daring. With *The Death of Argus*, in the Wallraf-Richartz Museum, Cologne, which was probably painted immediately after the *Descent from the Cross*, Rubens' 'Italianism' has returned, though the technique remains forceful. Possibly he was obliged at this time to execute commissions in a style closer to the taste of Antwerp than to his own.

The *Descent from the Cross* marks a return to a mode of expression much less free than that of the St Walburge triptych *(Pl. 43)*. A comparison of the two works in Antwerp Cathedral proves that, whatever has been said, Rubens' conquest of his own style was not a steady progression. This new commission, from the gunsmiths of Antwerp, on 7 September 1611, for their chapel in the Cathedral of Notre-Dame, seems not merely a return to more conventional formulas but a narrow submission to the iconography and spirit of the Counter-Reformation. Even so, it has undeniable grandeur.

Although the *Descent* was begun at once, it was not completed until 1614. The central portion of the triptych was delivered during 1612, and the side-panels on 18 January and 6 March 1614. Obviously during this time the artist was working on various other pictures.

Nicolas Rockox was instrumental in obtaining this commission for Rubens. The subject was decided by the members of the gunsmiths' guild: their patron, St Christopher, was to occupy an important position in the triptych. A synod which met in Antwerp the year before, however, decided that only Christ should occupy the centre of altar paintings. The saint was therefore relegated to the outside of the side-panels.

41 *Descent from the Cross*. Detail

The subject of the descent from the Cross had long been represented by painters according to fixed rules. For nearly two centuries paintings and miniatures had shown the Cross in the centre of the picture with one ladder leaning on each arm of it, and a man on each ladder supporting the body of Christ. At the foot, the Virgin Mary, the Holy Women and St John mourned. One man, Daniele de Volterra, changed all that. His *Descent from the Cross* in the Church of the Trinità dei Monti in Rome, painted in 1541, set a precedent with its architectural nobility and grandeur. The figures were multiplied, and the two ladders became five. Placed in deceptive disorder, in billowing clothes, men lower the body of Christ with dramatic gestures. In the foreground the Virgin swooning in the arms of one of the Holy Women displays, as Émile Male wrote, 'the lines of an Ariadne'.

The novelty and epic quality of this work caused a considerable stir, and set a new standard of treatment of this subject for the painters of the Counter-Reformation. In taking his inspiration from it, Rubens was in harmony with contemporary taste as well as with the Church's requirements.

The content of Rubens' painting is generally the same as that of Volterra's. Five men lower the body, two of them placed above an arm of the Cross. At the same time none of them touches Christ's body. He 'slips down', in Paul Jamot's words, 'like the long stem of a cut flower', as Mary Magdalene reverently holds one of His feet stained with blood. The Virgin, unlike Volterra's and those of his followers, stands sobbing, reaching towards the dead son whose body is to be brought to her, yet full of dignity. This was Rubens' response to the theologians who held that Mary, in spite of her pain, should not be shown as liable to weakness. Thus Rubens seems to be the painter of the new Catholicism, with its new social position, admittedly, but also with strict views on iconography. The time was approaching when he would throw aside all formulas and, without denying or infringing the authority of Rome, paint freely, guided only by his own genius. His faith and his love of earthly beauty would be reconciled in his impulse towards the Creator. Pagan or Christian, that is the essence of his Baroque style.

The *Descent from the Cross*, was irreproachable: its balance of figures and masses was recognizably classic. Equilibrium dominates; and its grandeur and scale do not give rise to the 'naturalistic excesses' of the *Raising of the Cross*, with its emphatically rendered muscles and its theatricality. 'Here,' says Fromentin, 'is a youthful seriousness, the flowering of a candid and studious maturity, which will fade, and which is unique.' What is admirable in this *Descent* is not just the harmony of contrasting colours and tones, or the gracefulness of the body of Christ slipping down onto the shroud in a flood of light; it is the painter's success in bringing to a traditional subject, painted with traditional technique and expression, a heroic conception in which the dynamic of the *Raising of the Cross* has been refined and raised to the spiritual plane. Instead of unbalancing the composition or emphasizing unusual attitudes, Rubens has given majesty to the Christ figure by surrounding it with weighty forms and heightened movement, and making it the focus of his curves and planes.

Despite the fact that the figures are firmly based on horizontal lines and on the ground itself, the drama seems to be taking place in space, unaffected by the laws of gravity. Hands do not touch, or barely touch, the body of Christ; and one wonders whether it is in fact descending or taking flight. Those who are lowering Him have the attitude of dancers. Only the group of the Holy Women seems to anchor the strange 'ballet'—in which nobility and grandeur vie with grace and elegance—to the earth.

These Holy Women occur again and again in Rubens' work. Blonde and beautiful, they radiate calm, and contrast with the strong movement of the *Raising of the Cross*. Possibly Mary Magdalene was Isabella Brandt. In any case her face is one of the most delicate and charming Rubens ever painted.

42   *The Visitation*

43   *Descent from the Cross*

The painting in the *Descent* is more regular and flowing than that of the St Walburge triptych. 'In spite of its effect of relief, the painting is flat,' says Fromentin. The side panels, completed two years after the central panels, and representing *The Visitation (Pl. 42)* and *The Presentation in the Temple*, are much less governed by the edicts of the Church. The severity and harmony of the picture they flank are laid aside; their lively colouring and lightness—despite the tendency to overwork the smooth effect—make them seem almost dainty by contrast. The scenery—an Italianate palazzo—introduces an unexpected note. The decorative effect is charming; and we are reminded of Rubens' admiration for Italian architecture and his many studies of Genoese palazzi. He emphasizes the beauty of the surroundings, the ornaments, the simple poses, in order to heighten the contrast with the severity of the central scene, placing a pretty, full-bosomed laundress with a basket of linen on her head behind the Virgin in Flemish costume, who is greeted by Elizabeth and her little dog. Rubens' love of a particular type of feminine beauty is the only unchanging element in this work, still torn as it is between the influences, rules and taste of Antwerp and his own temperament.

The outside of the side panels forms a single whole. On the left St Christopher crosses a river with the infant Jesus on his shoulder; on the right a hermit holding a lantern lights his way. Max Rooses noted that 'the outside of the side panels of the *Raising* is more sharply painted; that of the *Descent* is softer in treatment'.

In response to requests from numerous churches the artist painted, with the help of his studio, several versions of the *Descent from the Cross*. One of the most interesting of these was for the Church of Notre-Dame-de-la-Chaussée at Valenciennes. It is now in the Valenciennes Museum. Whereas in the Antwerp painting the body of Christ descends along the length of the winding-sheet like flowing flesh, in this one the rigid body leans forward, the legs pointing straight down, the torso inclined to the right, and the head resting on the shoulder of Nicodemus, who is standing on a ladder. On

44   *The Holy Family, c.* 1619

the left Joseph of Arimathea supports the victim with the help of a long white sling. The Virgin, in tears, holds out her arms to receive Him, while Mary Magdalene and another of the Holy Women embrace Jesus' feet.

In the Valenciennes painting, Rubens abandons the diagonal for a more stable composition and emphasizes the vertical lines. The tragic power of the picture, however, remains. In the *Descent from the Cross* in the Lille Museum, by contrast, the artist returns to the oblique movement which corresponds more nearly to the Baroque expression. The figure of Christ slips between the hands of those who are lowering him from the Cross; the head is thrown right back, close to that of the Virgin Mary who looks pitifully at the pallid face of her son, His mouth half-open, eyes upturned, forehead covered with scratches from the crown of thorns, hair and beard clotted with blood. This pathetic juxtaposition is not a mere theatrical effect but true to nature.

The Lamentation in the Berlin Museums is similar in style and treatment to the *Descent from the Cross* and dates from the same period. This small wooden panel, with a luminosity reminiscent of Caravaggio, is painted with bold and rapid brush-strokes. One has the feeling that it was painted without preliminary studies, at one stroke. The contrast between the mourning women shaken by storms of grief and the rigid corpse creates a tension through which Rubens' whole genius expresses itself.

45   *The Holy Family with Parrot*

At the same time as he was working on the triptych of the *Descent*, Rubens carried out various other commissions. A small altarpiece, *The Resurrection*, was painted for the memorial in Notre-Dame above the tomb of Jan Moerentor—better known as Moretus—Plantin's son-in-law and principal collaborator, who died in 1610. As for the *Jupiter and Callisto* in the Cassel Museum (signed and dated 1613), its companion-piece *Venus, Bacchus and Ceres* in the same museum, and *The Victory over Drunkenness and Lust* in the Kunsthistorisches Museum are part of a whole collection of 'academic' paintings whose subjects and treatment suggest Rubens' complete agreement with the bourgeois taste of Antwerp society. He flattered his admirers by his smooth execution of well-balanced compositions, with harmoniously distributed colours and transparent shadows. *Cupid making his Arrow*, in the Schliessheim Museum, is an imitation of a painting of this subject by Correggio in the Kunsthistorisches Museum, though without Correggio's softness; in *The Holy Family* in the Pitti

46   *Flight into Egypt*

47 *Susanna and the Elders*   48 *Susanna and the Elders*

(Pl. 44) and *The Virgin with Parrot* in Antwerp—unfortunately repainted and added to—the peaceful, everyday realism of Aertsen, occasionally enlivened by the more dramatic influence of Caravaggio, is visible. This is true of many canvases produced by Rubens during this period.

Not very different in manner from *Jupiter and Callisto* and its companion, *Venus, Bacchus and Ceres,* is the *Hero crowned by Victory* in the Cassel Museum. It was originally hung above the fireplace in the meeting room of the Serment de l'Ancienne Arbalète in Antwerp, and contains the handsome torso of a blonde woman seen from behind. This is Rubens' ideal female figure, inspired in this case by *The Bacchante* of Annibale Carracci in the Uffizi.

The *Flight into Egypt*, also in the Cassel Museum, again shows the Italian influence—tempered, however, as Antwerp preferred it, by a freedom and realism which can be observed both in the lighter

103

tones of the painting—the yellowish ochre of Joseph's cloak, the bright blue of the Virgin's mantle, the lively red of the angel's clothes—and in the vigorous treatment of the shadowed portions. The small wooden panel showing the same subject, which belongs to the Gulbenkian Foundation in Lisbon and is almost certainly a sketch for a third work painted at this time and then lost, is more even in tone and more swiftly executed, although it is similar to the *Flight into Egypt* at Cassel. Some historians have tried to make out a case for a relationship between this sketch, in which the landscape is given more importance than in the Cassel painting, and where there are apparently several sources of light, and two paintings in the Louvre and the Munich Pinakothek, in which the German painter Adam Elsheimer has also represented the flight into Egypt. Rubens was friendly with Elsheimer in Rome, and temporarily influenced by him. Learning of his death in 1610, he wrote to his friend Dr Johann Faber in Rome saying that he would be glad if Elsheimer's *Flight into Egypt* were to fall 'into the hands of one of my compatriots, who should bring it here'. He would have found it deplorable had no Flemish collector possessed a work by the dead painter. 'I shall take particular pains,' he adds in a postscript, 'over the sale of this work.' So the painting may have inspired the Gulbenkian sketch and the corresponding finished work.

Among the major works also carried out in 1614 must be mentioned a small painting on wood, in the form of a sketch: *Susanna and the Elders*, in the National Museum, Stockholm *(Pl. 48)*, besides the *Pietà* in the Kunsthistorisches Museum and the *Venus frigida* in Antwerp *(Pl. 49)*.

Rubens had already treated the Biblical subject of Susanna and the elders—first during his stay in Rome, then on his arrival in Antwerp (in San Fernando Academy, Madrid). The Stockholm painting, one of the few works signed and dated by the artist, shows Susanna, her skin like mother-of-pearl painted fluidly, lustrously, seemingly enamelled, seated on some red material with her feet in the water

49 *Venus frigida*, 1614

of a spring. Surprised by the elders, whose heads and hands are seen against the light and sketched in with rapid strokes in some thin and transparent paint, she is turning hastily and trying to cover her thighs with a white sheet. Four years later Rubens offered Sir Dudley Carleton a painting of the same subject by one of his pupils, improved and added to by himself.[37] This *Susanna*, very different from the previous one, is perhaps the one now in the Hermitage. Another, painted in 1636, belonged to the Duc de Richelieu and is now in the Munich Pinakothek. De Piles' critical comments on it appear in his description of Richelieu's treasures, which included a famous collection of works by Rubens.

There was a sixth *Susanna*, which is lost; all that remains of it is Lucas Vorsterman's engraving, considered by Rubens to have been the best one ever done from his own paintings. Manet, according to Charles Sterling[38], took from the pose of Susanna his inspiration for the young woman in his *Nymphe surprise*, the only fragment of which is now in the Museum of Buenos Aires: she is facing in the opposite direction to the Susanna of the engraving. It is not known whether Manet saw the original, or a copy of it, or simply the engraving.

The *Venus frigida*, or *Freezing Venus*[39], in the Antwerp Museum, seems as traditional as other paintings of this period. No daring stroke upsets its harmony. The figure of the goddess, imitated from the famous *Crouching Venus* sculpture in the Vatican, is painted in full light, smoothly, with a softness which emphasizes the transparent quality of the shadows. Tschudi has pointed out that the landscape background, an unskilful piece of work, is an eighteenth-century addition.

Rubens' household now contained two newcomers: Clara-Serena and Albert, born in 1611 and 1614. The artist was supervising the building of his studio, which would enable him to leave his father-in-law's attic where he worked until 1617 or 1618. His reputation, his fortune, and the number of his commissions all continued to grow. His warm and open style, at once sensitive and robust, became more pronounced, though it did not overstep the bounds of fashionable taste and convention. The only thing which cast a shadow over this period was the death of his brother Philip at the age of thirty-eight, in the very year of Clara's birth. They had always been very close. Philip had recently married Marie de Moy; they had a daughter who bore the same name as Rubens' daughter; and the two fathers were godfathers to each other's children. A few months after her husband's death Marie gave birth to a second child, who was christened Philip after his father.

Rubens' vast output during this period of his maturity (about his fortieth year) raises the question: how much of it is to be taken seriously? For Rubens himself it was easy to pass from one commission to the next, and from one *genre* to another. Nevertheless he

50   *Doubting Thomas*, 1615

was fully aware of what he was doing. He was the slave neither of his princes, nor of Antwerp society. He was biding his time. He was also perhaps seeking to show his contemporaries that it was possible to work to one's full capacity even within strict limitations; he was beating them at their own game.

To defy society in an age in which a painter is both a courtier and a civil servant is dangerous. But Julius II was powerless against the genius of Michelangelo even whilst beating him with a stick on the scaffolding of the Sistine Chapel. Even the snickering of the canons—'bestiale e fantastico!'—at the undress of St Matthew and the physical beauty of the angel in the Contarelli chapel in San Luigi dei Francesi was no more than a foretaste of the hour when its sarcasms at the expense of *The Nightwatch* would deprive arrogant Amsterdam of the dark prophet of the Judensbreedestraat; of the insults to Courbet's *Baigneuses* and Manet's *Olympia;* of the damnation of Van Gogh and the isolation of Cézanne.

Rubens bided his time. The *Raising of the Cross* had been a sign, though a premature one. When he had exalted his own Creator, when his geniuses were gods and his men heroes, and when all had become one vast epic, no one would be able to resist him—no sovereign and no church. Rubens would seize life with both hands; not as a revolutionary, but like a demiurge. He would enter his terrestrial Eden.

The only known painting which bears the date 1615 is *Doubting Thomas* in the Antwerp Museum *(Pl. 50)*. It is a triptych, whose side panels represent Nicolas Rockox and his wife Adrienne, née Perez. These two died in 1640 and 1619 respectively, and the picture adorned their tomb in the Church of the Minorites in Antwerp. It is just possible that the triptych was not originally conceived as such, and that the Burgomaster had the portraits added later.

A comparison of these traditional paintings with *St Francis receiving the Stigmata*, belonging to a private collection in Brussels, is particularly instructive. This sketch, whose rapidity, brio and interior tension are most striking, does not correspond to any known painting or engraving; but it is possible that it was done for the Capuchins, with whom Rubens had continuous relations. The Reverend Father Hildebrand[40], the Order's archivist, has discovered that there was at one time a question of commissioning a large altar painting for their church in Antwerp, but that a letter from the General of Capuchins, Father Paolo da Cesena, dated 10 March 1617, condemned as excessive the price of 400 ducats. This letter mentions neither subject nor artist; it does, however, observe that the painter has already under-taken large altarpieces for the Capuchin churches of Cambrai and Lille, and we know that these paintings were by Rubens. At all events, the Antwerp project was not pursued.

The qualities of the *St Francis* picture are present in *The Martyrdom of St Ursula* in the Brussels Museum. With a minimum of preparation, the artist has outlined the figures with swift brush-strokes, establishing the rhythm of the whole, and developing all areas simultaneously. Then, with the same sureness of touch, now tense, now caressing, he has defined the figures; not by their outlines, but from within, making them more compact and firm. Side by side the colours are heightened, the lighter parts emerge from the shadows, and animation appears, without compromise to the fluidity of the whole. Rubens has thought in form and colour, and modelled in living flesh. In this tumultuous composition he nevertheless remains rigor-ously economical in his means of expression: the dramatic intensity of the massacre of the eleven thousand virgins by the Huns is rendered by less than a dozen figures. But it is not only his convincing power of illusion that proves his genius; it is the tremendous force and torrential movement of his figures. This painting is one of the first songs of triumph of Rubens' Baroque style.

The three paintings of the Magi, *Gaspar, Melchior* and *Balthazar*[41], were commissioned by Balthazar Moretus for the Plantin press at the same time as were the portraits destined to adorn the famous house in Antwerp where they are today. The persons represented are Christoph Plantin, Jan Moretus, Justus Lipsius, Plato, Seneca, Leo X, Lorenzo de' Medici, Pico della Mirandola, King Alfonso of Aragon, and Mathias Corvinus, the learned King of Hungary. To these were added other members of the Plantin-Moretus family, whose custom it was to name the three eldest sons of each generation after the three Magi. Among the accounts of the famous printing works one finds payment due to Rubens: 'For five portraits on panels, namely Our Lady with the Infant Jesus, St Gaspar, St Melchior and St Balthazar, for the account of Balthazar Moretus, at thirty florins apiece, val. 150.' The pictures of the Magi were probably removed from the Plantin establishment during the eighteenth century.

These various portraits, correct but frigid, bear witness to the 'soigné' style Rubens adopted to please his clientèle. His assistants undoubtedly had a hand in the pictures. By contrast, it is to himself alone that the splendid portrait of Muley Ahmad can be attributed. The subject was the Bey of Tunis' son; it was sold at the Radstock sale in London in 1826 as 'Tamerlane'. The painting now belongs to the Boston Museum of Fine Arts.

Although the *Four Negro Heads (Pl. 57)* is of later date (about 1620) it is useful to compare it with the masterpiece just cited. This painting was stolen from the Brussels Museum in 1964, and recovered a few weeks later. In it are revealed all Rubens' strength and suppleness of touch, as well as profound psychological insight. Painted in scumbled patches which overlie and obliterate each other or appear side by side, according to the physiognomy of the subjects, the faces are taken from life, and modelled in warm and cold tones simultaneously. Coppery red, ochre, grey and blue harmonize admirably and without excessive richness. This is the work of a virtuoso free from the limitations imposed by commercial considerations: skilful, intelligent, masterly. Face to face with his model, the painter has at once understood him and found the technique and colouring best fitted to express his understanding. In the large paintings commissioned for churches, civic bodies and palaces, he orchestrates and conducts; he is the supremely fertile studio manager distributing paintings wherever they are required. His hand is everywhere, but never alone. Later, having firmly established his style, he abandoned the conventions of Antwerp and put an end to what he called his 'manufactory of paintings'.

The model for the *Four Negro Heads*, one of the Negroes who landed at Antwerp in one of the ships docking there, posed for several other painters at the same time. One finds him in canvases by Jordaens and Van Dyck, amongst others. It was to Van Dyck, indeed, that the Rubens painting was attributed in the exhibition 'Rubens and his Time' at the Orangerie des Tuileries in 1936. In 1965, however, in the exhibition organized by the Royal Museums of Brussels, under the title 'The Century of Rubens', it was attributed to him. 'For psychological reasons, and because of certain stylistic observations, we are attributing this work to Rubens,' wrote M. Leo van Puyvelde in his notice. It appears that Rubens alone at this period had achieved the ambition of so many painters; to paint a soul in a face.

51 *The Sufferings of the Church*

The *Christ à la Paille* in the Antwerp Museum, and *Christ giving the Keys to St Peter* in the Wallace Collection are probably contemporary, dating from 1617 or 1618; but the first is painted with greater freedom than its rather dull and academic counterpart. This was commissioned by Nicolas Damant, chancellor of the sovereign council of Brabant, and placed above a small altar to the right of the entrance to the chapel of the Holy and Miraculous Sacrament in the Church of St Gudule in Brussels. The altar and painting were intended as a monument for the chancellor and his wife and family. The historian Georges Forster declares that it is the most beautiful Rubens he ever saw; Reynolds on the other hand—though he admired Rubens' 'flowery, spontaneous, loose and careless style'—treats the picture somewhat disdainfully.

The *Return from Egypt*, which belongs to the Earl of Leicester's collection at Holkham Hall, was for a long time thought to be a copy of the painting in the Hermitage; but the contrary is certainly the case. Among other works of this period are the portraits of the Archduke and Archduchess, which were sent by their sitters to the Marques de Sieste-Yglesias, and are today in the Prado.

The Wallace Collection in London contains a *Holy Family* which comes from Archduke Albert's oratory and was painted probably about 1614-17. The critic Thoré-Burger pronounced this work 'fresh, vermilioned, full-blown... a masterpiece of its kind'. In the same style, and from the same period, are the *Virgin with the sleeping Child* in Munich; the *Descent from the Cross*, painted for the Capuchin church at Lier and now in the Hermitage; and *Christ in Simon's House*, also in the Hermitage. The last-named painting, formerly in the Duc de Richelieu's collection, was described by de Piles in exalted terms: 'The manifestations of human passions in this work are striking, particularly those of Mary Magdalene who, amidst all her torrents of tears, shows the excess of her love... I have seen all that is splendid of Titian and Giorgione in France and Italy; but nothing has touched me like the power of this painting.'

52   *The Flagellation*, 1617

Other notable works of the period include *Christ and the Adulteress*
and *The Massacre of the Innocents* in the Brussels Museum; *The Child
Jesus with St John and two Angels* in the Kunsthistorisches Museum,
of which there are fine copies, probably by Rubens himself, in the
Berlin Museums and the Pembroke collection at Wilton House;
the *Virgin with a Basket* in Potsdam Schloss; the *Tribute Money*
in the Young Museum in San Francisco; and the *Adoration of the
Magi*, painted for the Capuchins of Tournai, and now in the Brussels
Museum.

53 The Holy Family

The Flagellation, in the old Dominican Church of St Paul of
Antwerp, is a powerful work, carefully finished; its colouring is dull,
and in places pale. The date, 1617, on the outside of the side panels,
was added during the last century and is probably not that of this
painting but of the completion of the series of fifteen paintings
representing the mysteries of the Rosary which were commissioned
from various artists. These pictures still occupy one of the side-
aisles of the church, but Rubens' picture, which is superior to the
others, has been replaced by a copy and removed to a position near
the altar *(Pl. 52)*.

A few portraits of Antwerp bourgeois mark these years of research, during which Rubens did not disdain, for the sake of pleasing his rich and pious clientèle, to paint Madonnas with children which his friend and collaborator Jan Brueghel, son of Peter Brueghel the Elder and nine years Rubens' senior, surrounded, in accordance with the fashion of the time, with garlands of flowers. This is the case with *The Madonna and Child with a Garland* in Munich, *The Madonna with a Garland* in the Louvre, and *The Madonna with Forget-me-nots* in Brussels. Clearly Rubens, for friendship's sake, tried to accommodate his style to that of Brueghel, though his efforts were not always appreciated. 'Master Rubens,' writes Brueghel to a confidant of his protector Cardinal Borromeo, 'has also done his best to demonstrate his powers in the central picture, (*The Madonna with a Garland* in the Louvre), which contains a very beautiful Madonna.'

The friendship between the two painters was unflawed. On Rubens' return from Italy he found his senior contemporary, heir to a glorious line of artists, in the full flower of his powers and fame. Brueghel

54　*The Holy Family, c.* 1638

too was court painter to the Archduke and his wife, and this is probably why they joined forces. In 1610 Rubens painted Jan Brueghel and his second wife Catherine van Marienburg. A few years after this Brueghel had his father's monument built in the chapel where he lay buried, in Notre-Dame in Brussels. At his request Rubens made a replica of the St Gudule *Christ giving the Keys to St Peter*, which is now in London. The second version, sold in 1706 and replaced by a copy, is at present in the E. R. Bacon Collection in New York.

A further expression of Rubens' friendship with Brueghel is a family portrait in which the latter appears with his wife and two children in the best Antwerp tradition of portraiture; substantial and somewhat stilted. This painting is in a private collection in London.

55 *Adam and Eve*

56 Rubens and Jan Brueghel, *Adam and Eve in Eden, c.* 1620

In 1615 Isabella Brandt stood as godmother to one of Brueghel's daughters. He himself never showed a trace of jealousy towards his younger friend. Writing to Cardinal Borromeo, in 1624, he declared that Rubens was 'fortune's favourite; to such an extent that he has received more honours and riches than any other artist of our time'. When Brueghel died of the plague on 12 January 1625, Rubens wrote his epitaph in the Church of St George in Antwerp and decorated his tomb with a portrait of his friend. This was lost during the Revolution.

The collaboration of the two painters was a considerable one. In the studio in the Wapperstraat, Brueghel was the specialist in flowers, fruits and animals. In *Adam and Eve in Eden* (Mauritshuis, The Hague), painted about 1620, only the figures are by Rubens. It is signed on the left: PIETRI PAULI FIGR.; and on the right:

J. BRUEGHEL FEC. Brueghel is responsible for the birds and animals which appear in the landscape. They are finely and meticulously rendered, in contrast to the full-bodied medium of Rubens. However there is no disharmony between the supple rhythms of the two figures and these creatures. The subtly balanced interplay of light and shade gives a remarkable unity of impression *(Pl. 56)*.

Although influenced by Rubens, whom he admired, Brueghel retained his own style, which was characterized by extreme care for detail. This was designed to render with great exactitude the variety of plants and animals. His master, for his part, saw the whole rather than its parts.

The double monogram of the two painters appears on the *Diana* in the Augsburg Gallery, which Rubens kept, like *Adam and Eve in Eden*, in his studio until his death. About 1617-18 he painted, this time alone, the same subject on two very similar canvases. These are now in the Paul Getty Collection and in the Cleveland Museum of Art.

It was accepted at this time that two painters might collaborate on one canvas, each undertaking the portion in which he specialized. Rubens did as his contemporaries did; but his unique talent and mastery and his ascendancy over them soon distinguished him. In Antwerp he became the 'coach' of his admirers and followers. He respected Jan Brueghel to the point of supplying figures for his paintings, but he also encouraged and helped Snyders to perfect his style, saved Brouwer from destitution, and bought paintings from other colleagues which he kept in his collection.

His reputation increased yearly. At the same time his competence grew, and he began to feel capable of imposing his own style when the chance arose. Alone from now on he would face Antwerp, where he was famous, and go beyond its confines to conquer the foreign courts he had made contact with in Mantua, Rome, Valladolid and Madrid. His first gesture was to get rid of the numerous pupils and collaborators he had needed to fulfil his many commissions;

and he was pleased to take the opportunity offered to him in 1618 of getting off his hands a number of paintings carried out with their help by selling them to Sir Dudley Carleton in exchange for a collection of antiques. The year is a key one both for Rubens' work and for his life.

His change of attitude was foreshadowed a year before this, in an admirable triptych: *Christ à la Paille*, painted for the tomb of Jan Michielsen, an Antwerp merchant who died on 20 June 1617, and placed in the Cathedral before finding its way to the Antwerp Museum. The left-hand panel shows the Virgin and Child, and on its reverse there is a monochrome sketch of the Saviour. The right-hand panel is of St John the Evangelist; on its reverse there is another sketch of the Blessed Virgin. Only these sketches are the work of a pupil; the whole of the rest is by Rubens himself *(Pl. 58)*.

According to Oldenbourg, *Christ à la Paille* was painted by Van Dyck; however, there is no proof that he was working with Rubens at this time, nor do his paintings of the period show any of Rubens' influence. The master of Antwerp must therefore be reproached with the 'weaknesses' which Leo van Puyvelde observed in this masterly work: 'Excessive realism,' he says, is the result of 'an exaggerated determination to confront reality in the slack flesh of Christ and the clot of blood at the nostrils which is made with a blob of vermilion mixed with carmine.' But the flaccid, livid corpse with its dishevelled hair and beard, the eyes turned inward and the arms swinging, is not just a fine piece of painting, supple and generous in its forms; it shines with a spirituality which is absent from the conventional works which Rubens had been producing for several years.

The artist has induced emotion not by displaying horror, but by finding the mysterious quality of the divine, before which men may kneel and pray. An intellectual process, but one which renders skilful brushwork and harmony of colouring more than a series of happy accidents and masterly strokes. This is success in the service of an idea, and it contains the truth of a noble pathos. The astonishing thing is that this corpse 'lives'; despite the laxity and pallor of the inert flesh, it trembles; the light that plays on it is that of the dawn, not of the tomb.

To what influences Rubens' development is due can never be fully answered. Born a Fleming, nourished by the Italians, established as the official court and ecclesiastical painter in Antwerp, he showed at the same time what could be done in the taste of the period and what he himself could do. He had to win a place in that society, however, before he could risk offending important people by freeing himself from contemporary conventions. With *Christ à la Paille* he achieved the truest emotion, springing from an observation of life. The piteous face of this Saviour possessed a realism from which most painters would have shrunk, and a living quality—despite its corpse-like abandon and livid pallor—of astonishing and 'scandalous' intensity. This was the power and glory that on the third day would triumph over death.

Tearing the veil aside, Rubens carried out in a few months those shattering operatic finales, the two *Last Judgments* and the *Fall of the Damned* in Munich. De Piles' pronouncement shows how the artist's development was interpreted in the seventeenth century: 'Rubens at first decided to follow the styles of Michelangelo and Caravaggio, but finding they entailed too much laboriousness he evolved one of his own, more expeditious, and more suitable to his own genius.'

The Count Palatine, Duke of Bavaria, Prince Wolfgang Wilhelm von Neuburg commissioned the first of the two *Last Judgments* for the church of the local Jesuits. In a letter to Sir Dudley Carleton on 28 April 1618 Rubens, compiling a list of paintings he wished to sell, mentions a *Last Judgment* 'begun by one of my pupils after a much larger work which I made for H. S. H. the Prince of Neuburg'. The commissioned work was therefore completed and installed at this date. Besides this, a chronicle of the Neuburg College of Jesuits

57   *Four Negro Heads, c.* 1620

mentions the painting as being above the high altar of their church in 1617. The date of its execution can thus be fixed as 1616, the previous year *(Pl. 60).*

Probably completed soon after this commission, the *Small Last Judgment* in Munich is of the same character, but measures only 182 × 120 cm, whereas the other is more than six metres high, and is one of Rubens' major works. The inspiration of the famous Sistine Chapel fresco is evident; its enormous stamina certainly spurred the Fleming to break out of the confinement of Antwerp conventions. The trick of fate which led to the proximity to each other on the walls of the Munich Alte Pinakothek of the two Judgments, the *Fall of the Damned* and the *Fall of the Rebel Angels* (1620), shows how close Rubens' liberation came to being an explosion.

Scoring his canvas along two oblique and divergent axes with successive knots of human figures, which jostle, confront and tangle with one another in furious disorder, Rubens shows in the *Small Last Judgment* a dynamism which defies all laws and logic. The movement which raises this confusion of bodies expresses the richness and intensity of the genius which he expresses to the full in the Baroque painting of his triumphal years. Light from many sources sweeps over the human avalanche, while the distribution of warm and cold tints, faint and intense lighting effects, enhances the effect of tumult. The colouring is everywhere vigorous, and reinforced in the brighter areas by skilfully managed highlights in white.

The same movement can be observed in the *Fall of the Damned*, whose style is also similar to that of the *Small Last Judgment*, and which was certainly painted in the same period. The canvas is crossed from top to bottom by the irresistible jostling of bodies thrown into everlasting Hell. One can guess Rubens' sensual excitement as he cast himself into this expressionism after years of waiting and resignation. It is as intoxicating in its way as the unbridled joy of *La Kermesse*, or the lively sensuality of the *Garden of Love*. Its curves and spirals wind, undulate and whirl; the diagonals cut across the composition and cause it to oscillate; the colour escapes from the matrix of the drawing and enters into conflict with the lighting; and the brushwork becomes not simply rapid and powerful, but flashing in great strokes, defining the essential motif and unleashing the explosive harmony in which purples, oranges and greens dominate in exuberant vigour *(Pl. 61)*.

This genius whose powers led him beyond himself, but who could always reconcile them with his own temperament and outlook,

58 *Christ à la Paille, c.* 1618

was to astound first Flanders and then Europe. As Delacroix wrote later, Rubens shook painting to its foundations, 'by the hidden power and interior life he put into everything'. Yet there was nothing in his own wasted and enfeebled country to support such extraordinary vitality. Baroque painting in Flanders owes its very existence to the personality of Rubens, without which it could neither have come into being nor gained such a hold on Europe.

From this point everything in Rubens desired adventure, everything insisted on his breaking free. He was no longer able to accept his position as one of the most active painters in Antwerp: he was determined to be the one without peers, who could ignore the competition. Once a sketch was accepted he insisted on being free to carry out the work according to his own intentions.

This was the moment, then, when Rubens the good husband and father, the humanist, the pious believer, the court painter, ceased to be just these things but became something much greater—the demiurge of the flesh, history, mythology and the Faith. Yet he

59 *Hell*

60 *Last Judgment, c.* 1615

remained two persons. The earthly Rubens, lover of fair flesh, of comfort and honour and power and court life; and the spiritual one, the warrior of the Counter-Reformation and the herald of militant Catholicism. The first of these flattered princes, glorified their deeds, and delighted in tender-thighed Venuses and Junos with round breasts, revelling in paganism as in an earthly paradise, and exalting the physical life in ardent action. The second reached the heights of spirituality, not as a mystic but as a participant in the struggle; and his realism gave strength to adoration, judgment, martyrdom, agony, victory, triumph. He was always interested in conflict: of victims with executioners, of conquered with conquerors, of hunters with animals, of the saved with the damned. Or else in contrasts: the infant Jesus and the Magi, Susanna and the elders, Angelica and the hermit.

Yet Rubens was not an ambiguous painter, a Janus-head; he was a confluence of currents and purposes, and his language was that of borrowings, of techniques, of antagonisms, which is now seen as typically his own, and which speaks more directly to the eye than to the intellect or reason.

It may be countered that he was not without meanness, or that his ambition caused him to be vain, irascible and vindictive. He would not accept the slightest spot or scratch on his image, whether it was seen by the citizens of Antwerp, its Archduke or its Church, or by the rest of Europe. But genius has its flaws: Rubens liked money and fame at least as much as he liked painting, or was to like politics, or, on occasion, the pursuit of love. But his greatness and dignity and nobility were such that his failings are easily forgotten. Up to the age of forty he had patiently built up a harmony between his life and his work. Then, when the moment of his freedom arrived, he began to climb the ladder of greatness. The herald of the Baroque was to be at once the historian and epic poet of the monarch and the champion of the Counter-Reformation. In his eyes, church and throne were defending western values against Calvinism. The

61 *Fall of the Damned, c. 1616*

modern phrase, 'man of the right', perfectly describes Rubens, as his future politics were to show.

In 1614 he had received an affront which he did not forget. The Chapter of the Cathedral of Ghent had had the temerity to refuse his painting intended for the high altar of St-Bavon, whose Bishop, Charles Maes, had accepted the sketch two years before. After his death, the canons had allowed the business to drag on; and the new Bishop, whose reply Rubens had awaited, decided to cancel it. Rubens, furious, applied to Archduke Albert. In a letter[42] dated 19 March 1614 he brought the affair to Albert's notice, putting into his 'report' all his rancour and vanity.

Whether the Archduke, following this letter whose 'perhaps impertinent terms' the painter apologizes for, actually intervened, is not known. The affront to Rubens may have seemed an insult to himself: Rubens was his official painter. But on 10 February 1623 Bishop Antoine Triest—Charles Maes' third successor—ordered the sculptor Robert de Nole to undertake a large altar including a vast space reserved for Rubens' painting. It was placed there a year later. The cathedral archives contain the receipt for payment for the picture, signed by Jan Brueghel on behalf of Rubens: it is *The Conversion of St Bavon*. It still occupies the place for which it was first intended *(Pl. 85)*.

The commission of 1612 had been for a triptych ('tavola colle parte,' says the artist's letter to the Archduke—written, like several of his letters, in Italian). The sketch ('un dissegno colorito') which failed to please the Bishop is now preserved in the National Gallery in London. It is noticeably different from the finished work, whose dimensions, composition and spirit underwent a change in the interval.

Rubens' taste for intrigue, which in his case went with a courtier's ability to flatter and a slighted civil servant's love of recrimination, found ample opportunities in his dealings with Sir Dudley Carleton. Rubens' failings remained; but in his dealings with foreign diplomats and princes on behalf of his country he was nobler and less prone to meanness.

Carleton, His Britannic Majesty's Ambassador to the government of the United Provinces, was a clever and obstinate bargainer who had been involved in political intrigue since the beginning of his career as secretary to the ninth Earl of Northumberland. His chequered political life had brought him to an enviable position: he was a close friend of the Duke of Buckingham, with whose meteoric rise Carleton's fortunes blossomed. It was as Buckingham's nominee that he became ambassador to The Hague.

Protected by his diplomatic immunity, Carleton became a skilful dealer in works of art. He had begun his operations at his post in Venice, flooding the London market with antiques, ceramics, plate and jewellery. Part of his purchases, principally Roman marbles, were still on his hands when he went to represent Britain in Holland.

Rubens had left Italy in haste, bringing back with him no works of art. He was tempted by Carleton's collection. His flourishing fortunes obliged him to have a well-furnished house adorned with fine things. Why not Italian works of art? It was the fashionable thing. Probably, too, he was flattered to deal with the English Ambassador rather than the usual dealer, and this gave the objects an added lustre. He offered, on 28 April 1618, a list of works in exchange for the collection; giving the prices, and stating whether the pictures were done by him alone.[43]

The business was far from simple, and gave rise to a series of letters between Rubens and Carleton, who claimed that the number of original canvases offered was 'insufficient' and worth 'hardly 3,500 florins'. He suggested a payment 'half in pictures and half in tapestry of Brussels manufacture'. This suggests that he was not a great admirer of Rubens' painting.

'I am no Prince,' answered the artist[44], '*sed qui manducat laborem manuum suorum* [but one who lives by the work of his own hands]; and that is why I believe that in offering Your Excellency, for the

62　*Christ between the two Thieves, c.* 1615

whole sum of my debt, these pictures—originals or carefully retouched copies—at this advantageous price, I am dealing very honestly. Moreover I am prepared to accept any intelligent person's arbitration in respect of these prices.'

There is no cause for the surprise which some people have evinced at Rubens' discrimation between his own pictures, those retouched by him, and studio copies. It was quite normal in that age for a painter to have several collaborators, and to put a variable amount of work into any given picture. Rubens' carefulness in detailing the precise proportion, in respect of these paintings, proves his honesty.

His commercial sense has shocked certain people. Yet he was only trying to defend the marketable value of his paintings by not selling them cheap. His determination to stick to his price shows his consciousness of the value of his works—even those in which his part was minimal, provided that he believed them worthy of his signature. If the Ambassador must have tapestries, he would accept this 'so long as their value does not exceed 2,000 florins'. The rest —Carleton was asking the large sum of 6,000 florins for his collection—was to be paid in pictures. Rubens even suggested adding 'a small, pleasing, original canvas' painted by himself 'expressly for' the Ambassador.

The exchange of letters continued. Rubens was working hard, and was anxious that Carleton should know he was bringing his pictures 'as near as possible to absolute perfection'. He was nevertheless vexed that the other should prefer to complete the transaction with tapestries from a source quite foreign to that of his own works, and let him know it. In reply Carleton charged him to work even more closely at the paintings; and, to balance this perfidy, called him 'prince among painters and gentlemen'. This time Rubens ran away with himself. Was His Majesty's Ambassador mocking him? In any case, he was beginning to wonder how favourable the exchange would be to himself. 'To sum up: in return for enough marbles

63　*Rape of the Daughters of Leucippus, c.* 1618

to adorn a room, Your Excellency will receive enough pictures to decorate a palace, and tapestries besides,' he wrote to him, with a certain bitterness, on 1 June. The paintings were not, for the most part, by Rubens' own hand; the marbles were not by any means masterpieces. Sir Dudley Carleton sold the former at a good profit. As for the marbles, their purchase had the repercussions Rubens had hoped for: his collection began to be spoken of not only in Antwerp but abroad. His taste, and his care for his house were universally extolled.

Some years later the painter met Buckingham, now the most powerful man in England. He painted his portrait, discussed politics with him, entered into his good graces, and, through the miniaturist Balthazar Gerbier, the Duke's confidant and secret agent (a man no more to be recommended than Carleton himself), sold him his collection of antique sculpture. It is possible that Rubens had remembered that most of the pieces were not of the best period. In any case he was not averse to selling the lot, at a profit, to Sir Dudley's protector, since the former had been so prompt to sell Rubens' pictures—without making the least distinction between the studio products and the originals. Thus the long business came to a conclusion. No one lost by it: skill and determination brought each side a handsome profit.

CHAPTER SIX

The irresistible attraction of the Baroque

The two Last Judgment paintings, the *Fall of the Damned* and the *Fall of the Rebel Angels*, end the cycle of paintings inspired by Michelangelo, in which Rubens showed an obsession with death and the hereafter which disappears from his work at this point. He now launched into history with *The Battle of the Amazons* (Alte Pinakothek, Munich), in which tumult and vertigo become secular. This painting, in parts reminiscent of Titian's *Battle of Cadore*, is carried by a powerful movement, and there is something sensual about the wild impetuosity with which the figures struggle together. The sap of the Baroque rises; but the subtly handled tone values give importance to, and link up, the less emphatic portions of the painting. The figures are less definite than in the preceding works; the drawing makes contours vibrate instead of giving them precision. The luminous outline of each figure thus renders it part of the whole. An impression of strength and flexibility, which is due mainly to the fairly small dimensions of the panel (121 × 165 cm), takes the place of description. Rubens' virtuosity is astonishing. Alone, and without collaborators, he orchestrates and spreads out this battle; on the other hand, he collects and concentrates into a severely restricted composition the *Rape of the Daughters of Leucippus*, also in Munich *(Pl. 63)*.

The day that Hilaria and Phoebe, the daughters of the King of Messenia, were to marry Lynceus and Idas, they were carried off by their cousins Castor and Pollux from the wedding-feast. On this theme the painter might have abandoned himself to a display of high spirits. Instead, he has controlled the excesses of the Baroque

64   *Drunken Silenus, c.* 1618

65   *The Battle of the Amazons, c.* 1618

and found a calmer means of expression. He has carried the scene into the open air and given it a bright light and intensity and contrast of colouring. Then he has arranged hexagonally, in undulating curves crossed by diagonals, three of his favourite motifs: muscular horsemen in glittering armour, nude female figures in full bloom, and horses. But what is most remarkable in the painting is its rhythm: the calculated slowness of the gestures, like cinematographic slow-motion, harmonizes with the resistance of the brides to the violence offered them, and with the calm and balance of the composition with its dense masses. Opulent blonde female flesh, enlivened with the characteristic Rubens vermilion, contrasts with the dark muscles of the horsemen, and the bay and dappled horses. The scene is drawn boldly against a fine landscape in which browns, dark greens and blues climb gently towards a huge azure sky; and following a method dear to his heart, he has caused forms and colours to oppose and respond to each other without breaking the classic unity of the whole.

As in *The Battle of the Amazons (Pl. 65)*, Rubens is not simply telling a story; he is using a pretext to exercise his gifts. More remarkable than the movement or the touch are the exercises in style: the beauty of a naked female body twisting, as if swooning in a man's arms; a rearing horse; brilliant red drapery linking two figures; a gleaming cuirass; the muscles of an arm or a leg. It becomes clear with what enthusiasm Rubens has painted this masterpiece: beginning by covering the canvas with thin paint placed with light strokes, restricting the scumbling to certain areas, he has laid thicker paint on the more brightly-lit parts. His brush has slowed down and substituted reflectiveness for rapidity, balancing the values, regulating nuances and varying effects so that a certain gentleness surrounds this scene of violence.

The year 1618 saw the birth of the *Drunken Silenus* (Munich) *(Pl. 64)*; *The Prodigal Son* (Antwerp) *(Pl. 66)*; *The Banishment of Hagar* (Hermitage); *The Banquet of Acheloüs* (private collection, Milan); and *The Virgin presenting the Infant Jesus to St Francis*, painted for the chapel of the Tailors' Guild in St-Gommaire, Lier, where the side-panels remain; the centrepiece is in the Dijon Museum. In the following year Rubens painted *The Last Communion of St Francis* for the Recollects' Church in Antwerp; the *Adoration of the Magi* for St-Jean de Malines; and two large works for the Jesuit church in Neuburg: *The Descent of the Holy Spirit* and the *Adoration of the Shepherds*. In 1620 followed the sublime *Coup de Lance*, now in the Antwerp Museum *(Pl. 69)*.

66   *The Prodigal Son, c.* 1618

Rubens plainly delighted in the variety of these paintings. There is the carnal joy of pagan bacchanal, bathed in light, and rich in texture, of the *Drunken Silenus*[45], whose date is known from a note sent by Rubens' nephew Philip to Roger de Piles. There is the rustic emotion of *The Prodigal Son* with its fine still-lifes of farm implements and its superb animal studies, its atmosphere of toil in the Flemish peasant tradition—though Reynolds found its colouring monotonous. There is a symphony of light, with delicate nuances, and moving spirituality, in the Malines *Adoration of the Magi*. There is also the poignant gravity of *The Last Communion of St Francis*, which Fromentin described so admirably, but without noticing how much it owes to *The Last Communion of St Jerome* by Agostino Carracci in Bologna. This is a work full of pathos and fervour, reminiscent of

138

the severe yet demonstrative piety of Flanders under the Archduke: the dying man, naked, on the steps of the altar, stretches with all his wasted and trembling limbs towards the Host, blazing with light, which he is to receive for the last time.

'Nothing of him remains alive,' writes Fromentin[46], 'except his small and humid eyes: pale, blue, fevered, glassy, red-rimmed, dilated with visionary ecstasy. On his lips, blue with agony, the extraordinary smile of those about to die, and the even more extraordinary smile of the upright man, the believer, who hopes for and expects the end, runs to meet salvation, and looks at the Host as he would look at his God made manifest...' The painting was sold on 17 May 1619 for 750 florins.

67 *Boar Hunt, c.* 1618

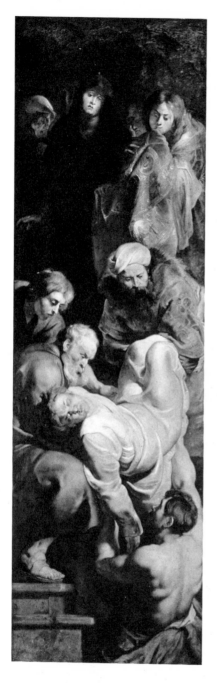

68   *St Stephen triptych:*
The Entombment (right-hand panel)

In this period Rubens painted several hunting scenes, with deer, lions, crocodiles, hippopotami, wolves, bears, boars, etc. All are full of wild movement, and contain savage struggles and epic combats. Their rapid execution combines with the splendid rhythms of their masses.

The *Coup de Lance (Pl. 69)* was painted for the Church of the Recollects in Antwerp in 1620, at the instance of Nicolas Rockox. The picture flames like a torch. There are careless portions in it, and weaknesses possibly due to unskilful restorations in 1824. There are also magnificent passages, in which Rubens reaches the heights of lyrical imagination.

One axis: Christ on the Cross. Two diagonals: the thieves bound to their crosses. The right-hand one is extended by a ladder which corresponds to the soldier's lance on the left. Around this the composition is made up of pieces set in juxtaposition, curves continually striking against angles. There is a chaos of shapes and colours, dispersed light, discordant gestures and poses. While the thieves writhe in torment the body of Christ is rigid and erect, as if about to fly, and bathed in impalpable light. The face is sunk on the breast. No suffering seems to mark Him, and He carries no tokens of death. The victim seems to triumph. Around Him mingle the figures, threatening or compassionate, of hatred, violence and sorrow. Like the other paintings of this period, it is entirely from Rubens' hand.

Several portraits date from 1618-20. The best of them seem to be those of Thomas Edward, Earl of Arundel, and his wife Aletheia Talbot, who are shown accompanied by a dwarf, a dog and a page. Rubens allowed himself to be entreated before accepting this commission. In an intermediary's letter to the Earl, Rubens' reply is reported thus: 'Although, says he, I have refused to paint the portraits of many princes and gentlemen of His Lordship's rank, I feel obliged to accept the honour he does me in asking for my services, for I regard him as an evangelist of art, and as the great protector of my profession.'[47] Rubens understood how to deal with great men.

69 *Coup de Lance*, 1620

Almost certainly Rubens painted the Countess first while she was visiting Antwerp; then, later, he must have added the Earl. He had already done a portrait of him in Spa in 1612, but this work is lost.

Also between 1618 and 1620, Rubens painted the famous *Chapeau de Paille* which is in the National Gallery in London *(Pl. 70)*. The model was Suzanne Fourment. This generously-proportioned young woman had perhaps little to offer in the way of character study; it was her beauty which attracted Rubens. She was the widow of Raimondo del Monte, and was married again in 1622 to Arnold Luden. Her father was Daniel Fourment, a wealthy dealer in tapestries in Antwerp. Rubens knew the family well; one of the sons had married Isabella Brandt's sister Claire. After Isabella's death, he himself was to marry Suzanne's youngest sister Hélène, who was hardly seven when this portrait was painted. Whether the splendid Suzanne, who often posed for Rubens, was also his mistress, is not known; it has been suggested.

In 1619 a humanist from Aix-en-Provence, Nicolas-Claude Fabri de Peiresc, a famous scholar, obtained for Rubens from Louis XIII, through the good offices of Gaspard Gevaert, Registrar of the city of Antwerp, a privilege allowing him to sell engravings of his pictures in France. This began a long friendship, marked by much correspondence, between the two men.

On 29 March 1620 Rubens signed a contract for the decoration of the new Jesuit church in Antwerp, St-Charles-Borromée, undertaking to deliver, before the end of the year, 39 pictures for the ceilings, the side-aisles and the galleries. The Fathers directed him to represent in them the harmonies of the Scriptures, themselves choosing figures from the Old Testament to correspond with the New: the visit of the Queen of Sheba to Solomon and the adoration of the Magi; Abraham's sacrifice and that of Calvary; Esther in triumph at the right hand of Ahasuerus and the coronation of the Virgin. The Jesuits did not object to this kind of symbolism; indeed, they introduced it into their new churches.

70　*Le Chapeau de Paille*.　Portrait of Suzanne Fourment, *c.* 1625

For this vast undertaking **Rubens** was authorized to obtain the assistance of collaborators—amongst them the young Van Dyck, then aged twenty-one—but the sketches were to be his own. He would receive 7,000 florins for this work, 'and on the same day a further 3,000 florins,' stipulated the contract, 'for the two large pictures of our Holy Fathers Ignatius and Xavier already painted by the same *seigneur* Rubens for the gallery *(hoochsale)* of our said new Church.' Owing to an error in translating the word *hoochsale* as 'choir' instead of 'gallery', which it means—and here specifically the upper oratory reserved for the Fathers—it was thought for a long time that these last two works were *The Miracles of St Ignatius* and *The Miracles of St Francis Xavier* in the Kunsthistorisches Museum. But the contract shows that the two large paintings had already been finished when it was signed, whereas nothing is said about the 'Miracle' canvases.

The contract provided for a single painting, for the high altar, of an unspecified subject. 'In case it shall be necessary to paint a new picture for the High Altar,' it reads, 'the Father Superior can order this from no one but the aforesaid Rubens, on reasonable conditions and subject to mutual agreement.' It may well be that this concerns the Vienna pictures, and that they appeared by turns above the High Altar.

Rubens painted two other pictures for the lateral altars of St-Charles-Borromée: the *Return of the Holy Family from Egypt* and the *Assumption of the Virgin*. These are at present at Holkham Hall and in the Vienna Museum respectively. It is worth noticing how little time Rubens took to finish and deliver the whole consignment: nine months.

But which are the 'two large pictures' which were painted for the upper oratory, at gallery-height above and behind the high altar? It appears certain that these portraits of St Ignatius and St Francis Xavier, founders of the Order of Jesuits are those now in the Brukenthal Museum, in Sibiu, Rumania. On 23 July 1619, Rubens mentioned

71 *The Assumption of the Virgin*

two engravings from these paintings, for which he was trying to obtain the grant of a privilege. This proves that they had been finished, as the contract says, before it was signed. They evidently served to decorate the special altar in Antwerp Cathedral at the time of the celebrations organized by the Jesuits on 24 July 1622 to mark the canonization of their patrons. The history of the portraits is known until their acquisition by Baron Brukenthal in Vienna at the close of the eighteenth century: it was he who added them to his collection in the Sibiu Museum.

Copies of the portraits were made by Rubens and his followers for various Jesuit churches and establishments. Those in the Vatican, attributed to Van Dyck, may have been painted by Rubens in Rome, in 1607-8, at the time of the beatification of the two saints. Like the Sibiu portraits, they were most probably used for some special celebration.

The decoration of St-Charles-Borromée, a magnificent marble building whose massive yet florid ornamentation bears witness to the splendour or the Counter-Reformation, was a task worthy of Rubens' gifts. He must have thought of the Sistine Chapel when he saw it. But St-Charles-Borromée belonged to Rubens' own epoch. It expressed the new and triumphant spirit of religion. Rubens too was modern; unattracted by the Middle Ages, he wished to express with his own style the daring and freedom of his age. He was to be a Baroque painter because the Baroque includes the sensual and the spiritual; at the same time he knew that it was only a fashion, and that art is not concerned with the transitory but with the universal. The Baroque was only a stage on the journey towards the new conception of life expressed by his forms, composition, colouring and technique. He was ideally suited to represent this surge into the future; his was a style for conquest, and it was taken up and propagated by the Jesuits in Europe. His encounter with their representatives in Flanders was of supreme importance in the ratification of his genius, for it was in St-Charles-Borromée that he first measured himself against contemporary architecture, and realized a series of works in direct relation to his own times.

Everything painted by him in St-Charles except movable works was lost in the fire of 18 January 1718. We only know from old paintings of the church interior that the pictures in the side-aisles were alternately oval, octagonal and quadrangular. Because of these indications it is possible to identify the sketches. A number of these belong to the Louvre, the Museum of Gotha, the Vienna Academy; others are in various museums and private collections.

In a letter dated 12 May 1618, Rubens let it be known to Sir Dudley Carleton that he was on good terms with the masterweavers of Brussels; and shortly after this, knowing the Ambassador's interest in tapestries, he offered to obtain for him the cartoons for *The Story of Decius Mus*, which, he said, he had 'just handed over to the chief of the establishment'.[48]

This series of cartoons, which are in fact oil paintings to scale for tapestries commissioned from Rubens by some Genoese gentleman belonged in the second half of the century to certain Antwerp artists; Gonzales Coques, Jean-Charles de Wit and J.B. van Eyck. At that time they were thought to be the work of van Dyck, painted from Rubens' sketches. As such they were sold in 1692 by the Antwerp dealer Marcus Forchoudt to the Prince of Liechtenstein.

During the last months of 1621 Baron de Vicq, Ambassador of the Archduke to the court of France, praised Rubens to the Queen Mother, Marie de Médicis, who was looking for a decorator for her new Palais du Luxembourg, built by Salomon de Brosse. The Archduchess Isabella was all the more willing to support the Baron's flattering opinion since she looked forward to having an unofficial source of political intelligence in Paris. She did not need to insist in order to make Rubens accept the enormous task which the Queen Mother intended to impose on him. He arrived in Paris in December 1621; the decision was quickly made; and he carried out, with astonishing virtuosity and speed, that combination of vital power and Baroque extravagance—and of proportion and harmony—known as *La Vie de Marie de Médicis*, consisting of twenty-one paintings in all.

72   *Education of Marie de Médicis, c.* 1623

CHAPTER SEVEN

A masterpiece of official painting

The Fleming now faced the Florentine, who was not only his
protectress's friend but the sister-in-law of his former patron, the
Duke of Gonzaga.   Their interview took place at the beginning
of January 1622.   A few weeks later Rubens began the sketches for
the gallery which had been allotted to him, in which he was to
illustrate the life of the Queen Mother.

She detested her son Louis XIII; she had rebelled against him
and her party had lost.   Removed from all power, she consoled
herself by building a sumptuous palace.   When his first series was
completed Rubens was to undertake another to the glory of Henri IV
—an amusing enough thought, since Marie had never had much
feeling for her husband, and had completely reversed his policies
after his death, giving the destinies of France over to the worst
sort of adventurers.   For the moment, however, it was with her
that he was concerned: a fallen monarch of forty-nine, fat and expressionless, an intriguer, sensual, and cynical, prepared now to use her
rebellion and its failure as material for a series of dazzling pictures.
In the twenty-four pictures—twenty-one compositions and three
portraits—in which Rubens, according to the contract of 22 February
1622, was to represent 'the history of the illustrious life and heroic
gestures of the said lady the Queen', an important place was to be
given to events which he himself would have preferred to pass
over in silence.   Marie, and more especially Richelieu, who was
rising steadily in the state, had their own intentions.

Nineteen 'devices' had been given to Rubens on signing the
contract: 'five more will be transmitted to him in the course of

151

the work,' said the document. On 19 May the painter brought the first monochrome sketches to the Queen. These were followed by studies in colour, some of them practically finished pictures, on oak panels measuring about 65 × 50 cm.

Marie de Médicis was aware of Rubens' good relations with the Archduke and, on his death in 1621, with the Infanta Isabella. Albert had indeed made his wife promise to make use of 'the great man of Antwerp as a diplomatic agent, and always to consider his advice'. Thus it was not only the foremost Flemish painter who was sent to Paris, but a counsellor whose shrewdness and suppleness of mind were already known to his employers.

Rubens was the first northern painter ever to undertake so large a scheme of decoration as that of the Luxembourg. At the height of his maturity he had been given a task normally reserved for Italian painters; and he must have thought at the time of the Farnese Palace he had so much admired in Rome. *La Vie de Marie de Médicis* is the only complete ensemble by Rubens which still survives, albeit in a different setting from its original one. The three others, unfinished, broken up or partly lost, were for St-Charles-Borromée (1620); for Whitehall (1632), and the Torre de la Parada (1636).

The twelve-year truce between the Catholic Low Countries and the Protestant United Provinces had ended on 9 April 1621. Philip IV had no wish to see it renewed unless the Scheldt were again opened to Spanish and Flemish shipping, and the Dutch withdrew their troops from the West Indies. These conditions were, on the face of them, unacceptable; but Maurice of Nassau, fearing another outbreak of hostilities, secretly told the King of Spain that, provided substantial indemnities were paid, he was ready to consider the return of the United Provinces to the Spanish Crown. The Prince of Orange had misjudged his countrymen's feelings: Pieter Peck, Chancellor of Brabant and the Archduke's envoy, barely escaped being lynched in the Hague, and the States-General unanimously refused to consider any *rapprochement* with Spain.

On 31 July 1621 Archduke Albert died. Isabella, that Most Christian Princess, condemned the war and demanded a new truce from Madrid, where only a military solution was considered feasible after the check with Maurice of Nassau. She hoped fervently that Rubens would be able to use his position in Paris to help bring about, through diplomatic channels, a renewal of negotiations. The painter, anxious to win favour in the eyes of Isabella and political reputation with his countrymen, was flattered; this would help him to become the kind of 'European' painter he wished to be. For Rubens there was no separation between himself as painter and citizen and Christian. His work lay in his public actions as well as in his paintings. He was, indivisibly, artist and diplomat, and might be considered the first 'committed' painter: committed, that is, to the cause of Catholicism in Europe, led by the courts of Brussels and Madrid, and by the Jesuits.

It seemed no descent for the creator of this world of the imagination—the almost superhumanly large and numerous and brilliantly-fashioned canon of his work justifies the term—to concern himself with the everyday affairs of men. Certainly no one took it ill, since his actions were so beneficial to his country, that he should have become the zealous servant of the king who had subjugated it. Besides, Rubens always distinguished between Madrid, whose methods he sometimes reproached, and the Infanta. He did not hesitate to warn her against the 'mistaken ideas' of the 'newcomers' in Madrid, whose bellicose attitudes so contradicted her earnest search for peace.

On 3 November 1622 he received the measurements for the first three paintings for the gallery in the Luxembourg. Seven months later, on 29 May 1623, he presented to the Queen nine compositions which he finished in their final setting. In February 1625 the scheme was completed. It was inaugurated in May, during the festivities for the wedding of Henrietta Maria, daughter of Henri IV and Marie de Médicis, and Charles I of England. To have completed such an

73   *The Exchange of the Princesses at Hendaye.* Detail, *c.* 1623

enormous task in less than three years, while at the same time working on other paintings and pursuing his political life, has led many people to assume that he was surrounded by collaborators; however, this was not the case, as can be demonstrated.

For his part, Richelieu saw at a glance that here was a great painter and humanist, as well as an ambitious man. The future Cardinal was aware that the Luxembourg paintings might be used in his own interests as well as to glorify the person of Marie de Médicis. In his delicate situation he was obliged to consider the necessity of consolidating his image; he wanted to be remembered as the reconciler of Marie with her son, rather than for the part he had played in her rebellion.

This was a somewhat paradoxical situation for Rubens, who thus found himself serving Isabella (and therefore Spain), by his political activity, and Richelieu by his art. For Richelieu, once in power, was to conclude with Calvinist Holland a military alliance—against Spain.

There is something extraordinary about the transformation, in these pictures, of the Florentine virago who did not love her husband but did her best to destroy his life's work, into the woman, mother and Queen, shining with all the graces and virtues, whose life under the magic brush of the great Fleming became a succession of felicities. This sort of transformation is common nowadays under totalitarian régimes, in which art is used as an instrument of propaganda. It was normal under the monarchy, and may seem less repulsive when we consider the greatness of the painters who were employed. And despite Rubens' surprise (which he hardly concealed) at some of the 'adjustments' he had to make, he was an official painter, used to glorifying Archdukes and Princes alike. In any case her contemporaries had less insight into the character and actions of Marie de Médicis than we have; and this was true even of Rubens. He was a court painter and could view his model only in the light of court art. He made a legend out of his subject, for this was required by the *genre*. What is amusing, perhaps, is that the legend was not invented by him but imposed upon him. It was an 'adjustment' of history, in the interests of power.

All twenty-one compositions were placed in 1953 in the former Room of State in the Louvre. This is one of the most magnificent decorative ensembles ever achieved, yet one cannot help having some slight regret that it was not left in the surroundings for which it was intended.

La Vie de Marie de Médicis celebrates the birth, education *(Pl. 72)* and character of the future Queen; then her marriage, and the birth

74   The Medici Gallery.   Louvre

of Louis XIII. *The Joys of the Regency, The Coronation of the Queen at St-Denis* and *The Apotheosis of Henri IV* are occasions for Baroque display into which allegory and mythology symbolically intrude. Marie's disastrous regency is the subject of a triumphal composition carried out by Rubens in a few days in order to replace *Marie de Médicis leaving Paris*, which it was suddenly decided to suppress. In a letter to Peiresc[49] of 13 May 1625 the artist recounts his having to supply another panel 'showing the splendours of the Regency and the blossoming of the kingdom of that era'. 'The subject,' he adds, 'has nothing to do with reasons of state, nor does it apply to any particular person. It does please greatly, however, and I feel that were I to be looked to and trusted, none of the subjects would have aroused the least scandal or censure.' And he adds in the

margin: 'The cardinal was somewhat slow to perceive these things, and was extremely vexed that the canvases should be taken so ill.' The letter continued in a rather disillusioned tone: 'I fear there may be many difficulties encountered among the subjects for the second gallery...'

In the study for the suppressed picture, which is preserved in the Munich Pinakothek, Marie de Médicis is shown being driven away by the demon of fury, while guile, with a fox on a lead, invites the queen to step into a coach. A lady-in-waiting kisses her hand, and in the air the hideous figures of hate and calumny gesture menacingly.

In fact, the Queen, exiled by her son, had left Paris under the roar of a mob incensed at her protection of the adventurer Concini, and had been lucky to escape bodily harm.

Politics also lay behind the celebration on another panel of the 'Spanish marriages' which Marie de Médicis had instigated: those of her daughter Elizabeth with the future Philip IV of Spain, and of Louis XIII with Anne of Austria.

The subject of the penultimate painting was, according to Rubens' instructions, to be *The Reconciliation of the Queen with her Son after the Death of the Duc de Luynes*. It, too, throws much light on the plans of Marie and her inspirer Richelieu. It was true that the Duc de Luynes had been Marie's implacable enemy, and had put an end, with the King's permission, to Concini. The Duc himself died at the time when Rubens received the Luxembourg commission, and this was a heaven-sent occasion for demonstrating the fortunate character of his death. He is represented on the panel in question transformed into the Dragon of the Apocalypse, struck down by virtue and courage, while Marie at last opens her arms to her son.

The Departure of the Queen from Blois gives historical truth a no less surprising twist. In fact, the Queen had escaped from the castle by means of ladders fixed to her bedroom window, which was quite high up. Being fat and far from agile, she had eventually to be wound in bedsheets and lowered like a bundle of dirty linen. She then crossed the town supported by gentlemen, to the amusement of night-walkers, who took her for a matron on a spree being assisted to her home.

None of this is, of course, suggested in Rubens' painting. She leaves her residence, whose door has been forced, calmly, responding with resigned lassitude to the cries of her partisans who brandish their weapons wildly. She is clearly a pitiable victim in the hands of conspirators whom she is too weak to resist.

A similar transformation has overtaken the battle of Les-Ponts-de-Cé, where Marie's troops were routed by those personally commanded by the King. Rubens has overcome the difficulty by mounting the Queen, proudly armed, on horseback, facing away from the battle in the background. It is extremely difficult to decide whether a

75   *The Imprisonment of the Queen, c.* 1623

76   *The Coming of Age of Louis XIII*

victory or a defeat is being represented, but fame and strength are certainly present at her side: one with a trumpet, the other accompanied by a lion.

Thus Marie de Médicis became, under the brush of Rubens, either the victim of odious machinations, or the implacable spectator of events outside her control. She, who was head and heart of the plot against the King, is here offered as a sacrifice to the enemies of France—whom, God be praised, her reconciliation with her son will plunge into the abyss as surely as it will rehabilitate her.

Neither the King nor the Queen Mother particularly wished to display the most painful episodes of their disagreements; on the other hand Richelieu, favourite and adviser first to the mother and then to the son, who had played a double game to win power for himself, saw that he could extract from these episodes a great deal of prestige as a conciliator. In fact he had delayed the reconciliation until he could appear in this role as the servant of order and peace.

Thus the instrument of personal propaganda, which this 'amended' history of her life was to Marie de Médicis, served Richelieu's own purposes equally well. Rubens accepted it all. He not only knew how to respect the caprices of governments; he knew that time was on his side. The series ends, astonishingly enough, with *The Victory of Truth*. Admittedly truth is represented leaping towards heaven, supported by the figure of time. This reminds us that time also settles many questions.

The King, the Queen Mother and Richelieu all declared their satisfaction with the work of the great Fleming, completed so swiftly. According to Rubens himself, in a letter to Peiresc[50], Marie de Médicis expressed her own pleasure 'on several occasions, and repeated it to whomsoever cares to hear it'. 'The King,' he adds, 'has done me the honour of visiting the gallery himself... His Majesty showed himself very pleased with my pictures. All who accompanied him assured me of this, notably M. de St-Ambroise, who explained the works, modifying their meaning with great skill when it was necessary...' Claude Maugin, Abbé of St-Ambroise, had certainly needed skill in the face of so many ambiguities. Unfortunately Rubens was unable to receive the royal visitor. He was in bed with an injury sustained while trying on a pair of shoes. It may have been a diplomatic illness. The painter confided to Peiresc that the accident, which caused him 'sharp, shooting pain', had obliged him to spend ten days in bed, which is rather a lot for a pinching shoe.

Rubens' enthusiasm could hardly have gone farther; nor could his technical mastery, eloquence of style, or ability to control effects. At first he had been less than inspired by the prescribed subjects; then he had seen that he would have perfect freedom of execution. He could mingle the past with the present, allegory with actuality,

77 *Reception of the Queen at the Port of Marseilles, c.* 1623

78 *The Taking of Juliers*. Detail

and history with mythology. He abandoned himself to his lyricism.
What he wrote to William Trumbull[51] was true: 'My talent is of such
a kind that, faced with enterprises of no matter what size and diversity,
I have never lost heart.' He spread out on the walls of the Luxembourg
an epic seething with life, sensual, heroic, full of warmth, peopled
with a young and graceful King, a Queen Mother full of opulence
and grandeur, and after them cardinals, princes, horsemen, lions
drawing chariots, horses rearing and galloping—a phantasmagoria
of forms and colours, where gods cleave the clouds and sirens surge
up from the waves, and there are trumpets and lances and the jostling
by torchlight of angels, allegories and heroes.

Everything Rubens has painted appears to be *natural*. There exist, it is true, certain exaggerations or awkwardnesses or chilly areas; but these are swallowed up in a flood of imagination and vitality. The painter's genius forces us to accept everything; even Henri IV, half-naked, sealing in mid-air his union with Marie de Médicis; even the dogs at her coronation at St-Denis. *The Reconciliation* is a strange pastiche of the pious imagery of the time, in which Rubens has literally obeyed her command to give the painting 'mystic qualities'. The Queen and Louis XIII are reunited in a mutual apotheosis which unashamedly evokes the celestial triumph of the Virgin and Christ. The winged genie smiting the dragon is St Michael himself, precisely as interpreted in the iconography of the Church.

Despite the dynamism of these paintings, the classical rules of composition have been rigorously respected. Each is based not on a determined design but on rhythms suggestive of movement which flow over the canvas carrying the principal elements. These rhythms stir the figures into a sort of swirl which unifies the composition. Only two or three fixed motifs are needed to anchor it and maintain its coherence. Forcing the Baroque impulse into strict limits, Rubens achieves *tours de force* everywhere, and his comparative carelessness when a subject fails to inspire him is more than made up for by his epic response to reality when roused.

The law of contrasts is applied equally to light and shade, to the disposition of mass and colour, and to the textures; it is applied to the orchestration, fraught with perils, of the real and the allegorical, which are linked by superb nude figures in the foreground.

These nudes act as carefully distributed 'counterpoints' in the work. Virtuoso of real and symbolic staging, Rubens is more than that when it comes to flesh: he kneads it as a sculptor kneads clay. Throughout his work, his love of a type of feminine plasticity is apparent; in *La Vie de Marie de Médicis* woman is everywhere, not only because this succession of pictures is a tribute to woman, but because she is the course and the grace and the warmth of life. Into the nudes of the paintings—allegorical, divine, mythological—Rubens puts all his unrivalled knowledge of relief. He does not underline form; he allows it to palpitate in a halo of light. Amorously he gives fullness to the flesh, makes it rich and supple; he rounds the haunch and makes the breast swell out, puts in folds and creases, multiplying curves. Splendid creatures as they are, they seem unfitted to bear the weight of clothing, any more than to suffer the constriction of a too-definite outline.

Veronese's theatricality, Carracci's carnal symbolism, and the sensuous splendour of Titian have all made their contribution to these paintings. There is little spirituality and less psychology in these faces. But there is tremendous energy throughout; it swells both the red robes of the cardinals and the majestic breasts of the goddesses. True or false, the Queen and her story interested Rubens very little. Once he knew what was required he let loose the forces inside him and allowed them to carry him away. This was not only a new age of painting but a new age for political man: the conscious triumph of absolute monarchy.

To return to the question of collaboration: how true are the suggestions which have been made?

When Rubens sent his first finished compositions for *La Vie de Marie de Médicis* to Paris, the Abbé de St-Ambroise pronounced a judgment which Peiresc hastened to communicate to the artist: 'At last he said that no one in Europe could bring such a vast work to a successful conclusion, and added that the Italians would take more than ten years to do what you would have done in four, and would not even dream of supplying pictures of such dimensions.' This appreciation reflects the opinion of the time. Rubens' speed of conception and execution was a talking point, and would later be embroidered upon with anecdotes of a 'revealing' nature, borrowed either from Sandrart, who first brought up the question of collaborators in his *Teutsche Akademie*, or from the Danish physician Otto Sperling[52], or from Roger de Piles.[53]

79 *Portrait of Anne of Austria, c.* 1624

Sandrart was acquainted with Rubens, but it is not certain that he ever saw him at work. He is not specific about the supposed collaborators. Otto Sperling, in his memoirs written at the end of his life, about 1670 or 1680, describes a visit to the studio in the Wapperstraat fifty years before, when work was going on at full swing; 'We also saw a large room without windows—the light came from a skylight. Many young painters were at work here at different pictures for which M. Rubens had made chalk outlines and indicated shades here and there, in colour. The young people had to paint these pictures, which M. Rubens himself finished with a few strokes and colours. All this was then described as the work of Rubens, and it is thus that this man amassed his extraordinary wealth, and was honoured with presents and jewels by kings and nobles.' This testimony, which is confused and vague, is manifestly aimed at injuring the Fleming's reputation. It seems to have inspired Roger de Piles to write, without offering any proof, that Rubens, too much in demand, 'had made from his coloured drawings, by skilful students, a large number of paintings which he afterwards retouched with the fresh eye, the lively intelligence and the quick hand which never deserted him; and thus acquired great wealth in a short time. But the difference between these pictures, which passed for his own, and those which were really the work of his hand, damaged his reputation; for they were, for the most part, ill-drawn and thinly painted.' On what grounds does de Piles affirm this? He produces no documents on the subject of Rubens and his studio; rather, he relies on his memory, or—as he wrote to the artist's nephew, who was also responsible for a somewhat questionable 'report'—'on what some men told me who were acquainted with him and who were witnesses to the things I learnt from them.'

De Piles was a limited man, incapable of understanding the impulses of genius. He begins with the observation that Rubens, having painted many canvases, particularly large ones, could not have been their only author. To support this notion, the painter's letter to

80　*Marie de Médicis, c.* 1625

Carleton of 28 April 1618 is often cited. In it, listing the works he desires to sell, he distinguishes with commendable honesty between those done by his own hand, paintings completed in collaboration, and copies. Three years later, writing to William Trumbull about a hunting scene which he proposes to repaint for Carleton, he returns to the subject with the words: 'entirely by my own hand, and without admixture of any other man's work.'

If any other evidence exists in Rubens' correspondence of the part played by certain collaborators in the execution of commissions, this refers to one short period in the painter's life, during which, while still searching for a style, he was working very hard to make a place for himself in Antwerp, and was showing little discernment in his choice of commissions. It must be strikingly clear that in his dealings with Carleton he was trying to get rid of old pictures painted in collaboration over the course of those years of experiment and research, during which his output was as abundant as it was varied.

In the contract dated 25 March 1620 between Rubens and Father Tirinus for the decoration of St-Charles-Borromée, it was stipulated that Van Dyck and other pupils of the painter's might carry out the work on the ceiling, but the sketches must all be by Rubens himself, who would besides be required to paint, alone, a composition for the high altar and for one of the lateral altars; the other would be furnished with a painting by Van Dyck. The affair was thus very specific, and one wonders why certain writers, among them Max Rooses, should have felt able to state that Rubens' collaborators, having finished the ceiling, shared also in the execution of the altar paintings which eventually numbered four. As in the case of *The Story of Decius Mus*, a study of these works reveals no hand but that of Rubens.

When he did collaborate, he said so; he saw no shame in obtaining assistance. In a letter to Jacques de Bie in 1611 he writes that he has 'had to refuse more than a hundred aspirants' wishing to work with him; but this was a case of young, inexperienced apprentices, who prepared canvases and colours and did menial work in all the studios of the day. If he had any more genuine collaborators, there is no trace of them after 1620 unless it be in the form of 'specialists' recognized by everyone.

In the major works of his maturity, as in the immense Luxembourg scheme, all intention, composition and expression is Rubens' own. His inimitable style proves this. If there is occasionally room—and this is inevitable in such a collection—for attributing to collaborators certain decorative portions or backgrounds or figures of secondary importance, the main work bears the general imprint of the man whose creative energy and virtuosity rendered him easily capable of bringing to a happy conclusion such vast areas of paint. His honesty and his scruples, of which there are plenty of proofs, were such that he would never have concealed another's share in a picture if this had been at all an important one.

For a long time it was believed that the monochromatic or coloured sketches made before the execution of large commissions were supposed to serve as guides to Rubens' collaborators; in fact it was for the clients' benefit that these were made, to give them a rough idea of the final work. Generally they were painted with astonishing swiftness and sureness. The sketches for the paintings of *La Vie de Marie de Médicis* were obviously done for the Queen and Cardinal Richelieu, since the completion of the series was, politically, too delicate a matter for each subject not to be precisely determined by those who were to profit from it. But the contract of 26 February 1622 is specific: 'Her Majesty further expects to receive no picture which shall not have been painted entirely by the hand of the said Rubens in respect of the figures, inasmuch as the said Rubens promises and undertakes to make and perfect all the above mentioned paintings.'

During the placing of the pictures in the Luxembourg the artist obtained the assistance of Justus van Egmont, of whom little is known except that on entering the Antwerp painters' guild he was

81　*Unseated Rider*

at pains to describe himself, like Guillaume Panneels, as a pupil
(shilder) of Rubens. This was also the case in 1621-22 of Jacob
Moermans, who remained equally unknown, but had the honour of
being charged in the master's will with the sale of his pictures after
his death, in conjunction with Snyders and Wildens. The family
paid him a thousand florins for his services.

This is evidence of the three painters' familiarity with Rubens, but
it is not known to what extent or when they collaborated with him.
The registers of the Antwerp Guild, and certain other documents
of the time, indicate that the painters Deodat del Monte, F. J. van
Branden, and perhaps the sculptor Fay d'Herbe also worked at
Rubens' studio; but for the first of these three, the date must be
distant, since he left Antwerp for Italy in 1612. This one learns
from a declaration made by the painter himself on the occasion of
the drawing up of a deed authenticated by a notary.

After his death there were many Flemish artists who arrogated to themselves the title of 'pupil of Rubens'. It is certain that the vast majority of them never worked for him, but all underwent his influence and adopted his 'manner'. It is in this sense that the 'title' should be understood: this permits a large number of men to share in the glory of the departed.

In the list sent to Carleton by Rubens there is mentioned a *Prometheus* on which Snyders painted an eagle. This is the only name mentioned by Rubens in connexion with collaboration by his disciples. Snyders, a specialist in hunting scenes and animals, appears again in the inventory of paintings remaining in Rubens' studio after his death: 'No. 168, a large piece with Pythagoras, and fruits by Franz Snyders.' One cannot conclude from this evidence alone that Snyders collaborated in numerous paintings by the master; and there is all the more reason therefore not to assume that certain Rubens paintings were painted by him.

The list also mentions the parts in several paintings played by Jan Brueghel, Cornelis Sachtleven and Paul de Vos, Snyders' brother-in-law. These are some of the specialists in various subjects such as animals, still-life, etc., whom Rubens occasionally worked with. The case of Van Dyck is somewhat different; although he was never, strictly speaking, Rubens' pupil, he was for several years his admirer and follower. This is why their works of 1618-20 have sometimes been confused; their styles in this period were quite close. There is, however, no proof that the words 'del meglior mio discepolo' which Rubens applies to one of the pictures he is offering to Sir Dudley Carleton, in a letter dated 28 April 1618, refer to Van Dyck. And although he is mentioned, notably in a letter to the Earl of Arundel from his secretary Vercellini, and in one from Toby Matthew to Carleton, as one of those who worked with Rubens, there is no mention of him as one of his old master's disciples after the year 1620.

Having glorified Marie de Médicis, the painter was to do the same for Henri IV; 'and in the said pictures,' stated the contract of

26 February 1622, 'to paint and present all the battles of the deceased King Henry the Great, his encounters, combats, captures and sieges of towns; together with the triumphs of the said victories after the manner of the triumphs of the Romans, and following the schema to be provided by Her Majesty.'

Rubens began, as he had done for the first series of paintings, with monochrome sketches for the King, his mother and the cardinal; but wishing first to complete *La Vie de Marie de Médicis*, he went no further than this. Difficulties had arisen between the Queen Mother and her architect Salomon de Brosse, and these are echoed in a letter to Rubens from Peiresc (21 April 1623). Was the delay in completing the gallery destined to receive *La Vie de Henri IV* due only to the negligence of the architect? It seems likely that Marie was in no hurry to see her husband celebrated as magnificently as herself. When Rubens, in Paris from February to May 1625 for the installations of the Queen's pictures, enquired about the progress of the second gallery, he met with evasions. 'I have the feeling,' he wrote to Peiresc[54] on 13 May, 'that there will be great difficulties over the subjects of the other gallery. They should, notwithstanding this, be easy to carry out, without any untoward incident. The theme is rich and abundant enough to fill two galleries; but the Cardinal de Richelieu, although I have submitted to him a written scheme in detail, is so busy with affairs of state that he has not had the time to glance at it.' The painter decided to return to Antwerp as soon as he had been paid in full for the first commission. If the Cardinal, now all-powerful, wished to take the initiative in asking him to undertake the second, he would be informed of this.

In any case his relations with the representatives of power hardly encouraged him to return to Paris and take up his brushes in their service. 'It is possible,' he added in a letter to Peiresc, 'that if they do not show the same punctiliousness in paying me as I put into the service of the Queen Mother, I shall not easily be persuaded to return.'

82　*Study of a Woman*

In the secret negotiations between Brussels and The Hague to try to reach some agreement, a young man, Jan Brandt, had for some years been playing a clandestine but effective part. He belonged to the Dutch side of Rubens' wife Isabella's family, and was her cousin. A confidant of the *stathouder* Maurice of Nassau (son of William the Silent and the magistrate Jan Rubens' ex-mistress, Anne of Saxony), he entered upon the scene at the moment when the Prince of Orange, having been forced by the hostility of the people and of the States-General to renounce his preparations for a return of the United Provinces under the Crown of Spain, declared himself in favour of a truce. It appears that when the Prince decided to inform the Infanta of his decision he authorized Brandt to get in touch with his cousin, whose relations with the Regent of the Netherlands were well known.

A letter written by Rubens from Antwerp to the Chancellor Pieter Peck on 30 September 1623 is generally cited as the first evidence of his political activity; but Rubens was surely engaged in affairs of state some considerable time before this. The Infanta Isabella, in an ordinance addressed to the military authority of the Steen at Antwerp on this very 30 September, directs that Rubens shall be allotted ten crowns' maintenance allowance per month *(diez escudos de entreterimiento)* 'without being obliged to present himself at muster inspection... by reason of his merit, and of his services rendered to the King, and in order to allow him to perform them with greater ease.'[55]

To be inscribed on the military payroll was a notable honour: such men were paid from funds sent from Spain for the upkeep of the royal army. Rubens' allowance was raised in 1630 to 20 crowns.

Jan Brandt—and it is worth noting that Rubens was entering into diplomatic activity as mediator between two of his own relations—had arrived in Antwerp to receive a reply from the Chancellor of Brabant (the Infanta's counsellor and Rubens' cousin), concerning the secret negotiations then under way, but he fell seriously ill. The painter, writing to Pieter Peck and referring to Brandt as 'el Católico', informs his correspondent of Brandt's reactions; how he has taken a note of the reply in his presence, and has promised to transmit it to the Prince of Orange. In addition Rubens asks for instructions concerning Brandt's presence in Brussels, which must be kept secret, especially from Cardinal de la Cueva, Spanish Ambassador to the court of the Infanta and extremely hostile to any agreement with the Dutch.[56]

We know little of these transactions in which Brandt and Rubens were not the only participants. Their secret nature presumably required the destruction of all correspondence. Philip IV, whom his aunt Isabella had kept informed, approved on 11 October 1624 Jan Brandt's proposal for a conference between the interested parties; but the death of Maurice of Nassau on 23 April following prevented the realization of this plan.

Madrid remained hostile to any sort of agreement between the United Provinces and the Netherlands. Even while negotiations continued the Spanish army besieged Breda, and on 2 June 1625, a few weeks after the inauguration of the Luxembourg gallery, Spinola, although in favour of an understanding with the Dutch, took the town. Its surrender was the occasion for Velazquez's masterpiece. But contrary to the hopes of certain people—of whom Rubens was one—the defeat did not have the effect of making the United Provinces sue for peace. Rubens wrote to Jan Brandt on 20 July[57] and on 25 August[58], with a view to resuming negotiations. Unfortunately these led nowhere and had to be abandoned. Without being a capital one, Rubens' role had been important: already on 30 August 1624 the French representative at the court of Brussels, de Baugy, was telling his government that the Infanta, faithful to the last precepts of her husband, often took Rubens' advice, and that ever-growing importance was attached to his words. This report, coming as it did at the moment when the artist was completing a monumental work to the glory of a government and country whose policies he was engaged in thwarting, can hardly have pleased Richelieu.

So seriously did Rubens take his diplomatic role, that he addressed to the King of Spain a petition for his own ennoblement, arguing that his dealings with the most eminent persons in Europe and his visits to their courts would amply justify such a step. On 5 June 1624 he received his patent of nobility and armorial bearings. The Regent of the Netherlands added the testimony of her own favour, appointing him a gentleman of her household.

From 6 September to 10 October 1624, King Vladislav Sigismund of Poland was visiting the Netherlands as the Infanta Isabella's guest. She asked Rubens, according to de Baugy's diplomatic report, to 'draw the portrait' of the King, 'in which I judge that his success will exceed that of his negotiation of the truce,' adds de Baugy, not without malice. This fine portrait is today in the Metropolitan Museum, New York.

During the summer of 1625 Isabella, who had gone to see Breda, over which the Spanish colours now flew, spent a few days in Antwerp. On 10 July she visited Rubens and authorized him to paint a portrait of her which is now in a private collection in Switzerland. The face of this noble lady of fifty-nine was familiar to Rubens, who had often painted it with that of her husband in official portraits. In this one, however, the Regent, representing His Catholic Majesty in his possessions in Flanders, is no more than a humble servant of God under the coarse material of the Poor Clares' habit she assumed in lieu of mourning on her husband's death.

Several other portraits of the Regent seem to have been painted at this time and in this costume; Ruben's style, if not his hand, is recognizable in many of them. The most interesting one belongs to Lord Aldensham; two others are in the Thyssen Collection at Locarno and in the Pitti Palace. The last, long attributed to Van Dyck, was identified as Rubens' work by Dr Ludwig Burchard. It is possible that several Orders of nuns, and particularly the Poor

Clares, wished to possess a portrait of the Regent in the habit of their Third Order. She wore it until her death.

At the French court several prominent persons had posed for Rubens. *La Vie de Marie de Médicis* consists of twenty-one compositions and three portraits: for two of these, representing the Queen Mother, 2,000 gold crowns were paid, according to Priandi, the Duke of Mantua's agent. The one in the Prado, acquired by Philip IV at the sale of Rubens' studio after his death, is well known. The body of the paint is smooth and fine, and the face has a fresh moistness of appearance. This does not succeed, however, in animating the heavy, expressionless mask of the sovereign, whose ample form is bundled up in capacious black robes. The studies for the succession of paintings celebrating her are more lively *(Pl. 83)*: for example a sketch in oils of her face, for *The Coming of Age of Louis XIII* (Munich Pinakothek), and, for the same painting, a red chalk and pencil drawing, highlighted with white (Victoria and Albert Museum). Two other portrait drawings of Marie, which were used as studies for the Luxembourg paintings, belong to the Louvre and the Albertina in Vienna.

The portrait of Anne of Austria *(Pl. 79)* must have been the companion picture to that of the King. They are faces of little interest in respect of the sitters' characters. As in *La Vie de Marie de Médicis*, Rubens worked in the spirit of court painting: 'classical' poses and compositions; severe harmonies occasionally relieved by brighter areas on faces, hair or details of costume; careful technique, without virtuosity or liveliness. The portrait of Louis XIII belonged to Kaiser William II before entering the Duveen Collection; that of Anne of Austria is in the Prado. The canvas in the Metropolitan Museum representing the Queen is a replica, not of the highest quality, but from the hand of Rubens. Later he was to paint another portrait of Anne, crowned, her face become somewhat gross. This is now in an American collection, and it is possible that it is the one mentioned in the inventory under the title: *Un pourtrait de la reyne de France régnante.*

83 *Marie de Médicis, c.* 1625

Rubens took advantage of Marchese Spinola's visit to the Infanta Isabella in July 1625 to paint his portrait. He later made several different versions of it to be given to the Regent, the sitter and his friends and relations. Three, from Rubens' own hand, are known to us: they are in the Herzog Anton-Ulrich Museum in Brunswick; in the St Louis City Art Museum; and in the National Gallery of Prague.

Richelieu did not appear to be in any hurry for Rubens to begin *La Vie de Henri IV;* he had every reason to distrust him, knowing as he did of his part in the Brussels negotiations. In any case France, in alliance with England, who was supporting the Dutch, was practically at war with Spain. As the months and years passed by,

Rubens saw the chances of his finishing this second scheme dwindling. Yet he did not give up hope, although the Queen Mother had not had the time, as he wrote on 20 February 1626 to Palamede de Fabri, Seigneur de Valaves, Peiresc's brother, to decide on the subjects of the paintings. Still, two years later he declared in a letter to Pierre Dupuy[59], a famous scholar and privy councillor: 'I have just begun the drawings for the second gallery, and I believe that the quality of the subjects will enable me to make it even more magnificent than the first. I hope to be able to show, through it, the growth of my talent...' Possibly Marie de Médicis had herself decided the subjects; but there is no evidence of the Cardinal's having approved or even seen them.

In 1625 in Paris for the installation of *La Vie de Marie de Médicis*, Rubens met the Duke of Buckingham, Charles I's intimate adviser and favourite, whom he was representing as proxy at his wedding with Henrietta of France. An unscrupulous adventurer, whose cynicism and audacity were such that he decided on the unceremonious conquest of Anne of Austria—'the gay spark overthrew the Queen and grazed her thighs with her embroidered shoes' wrote Tallement des Réaux—Buckingham asked Rubens, who was eager for the task, to paint his portrait.

It was his only chance of obtaining a close acquaintance with this important political personage. He did not wish to remain checked in the negotiations with Holland, and besides he felt that an understanding between England, whose support of the United Provinces he deplored, and Spain was necessary for the balance of Europe and a return to peace. The sittings were an opportunity for Rubens to express his views at the same time as discussing the sale of his collection of antiques, which Buckingham coveted. The conversation was rendered delicate by the fact that England and Spain were practically at war, though war had never been declared; and the breaking-off of the engagement of the then heir to the British throne to the Infant Doña Maria, Philip IV's sister, and the formation on his accession of the league against Spain (which included the United Provinces, France and Denmark), hardly predisposed the royal favourite to welcome Rubens' suggestions.

Two portraits were painted, and Rubens received in payment silver plate to the value of 2,000 crowns. One of these portraits, for which the coloured chalk drawing of the face in the Albertina, Vienna, was probably a sketch, is in the Pitti Palace *(Pl. 84)*. The other was at Osterley Park before its destruction by fire in 1940. This second picture was a state portrait, showing the Duke on horseback surrounded by allegorical figures; he was in black armour, gilded here and there, with a large brown cloak over it, floating behind him.

The ceiling of the staircase at Osterley Park was adorned with a very large oval composition known as *Apotheosis of William the Silent*, which certain historians saw as the apotheosis of Buckingham, though the face bore only a slight resemblance to those of the Rubens portraits. That this allegorical canvas, not in the best state, was by Rubens might be suggested by the fact that 'a picture of the Duke of Buckingham taken up into heaven' figured in the inventory of Rubens' goods. Such a work would have been painted in homage to the favourite after his assassination on 23 August 1628. The Lord Mayor of London, Sir Francis Child, acquired it in Amsterdam about 1697-99 and had it placed in Osterley Park, which he owned. The National Gallery possesses the sketch for this work under the title of *Apotheosis of William the Silent*.

On 6 June 1625 Rubens left Paris for Antwerp, where he arrived on the 12th. On the way he visited Brussels to inform the Regent of his conversations with Buckingham. On 10 July Isabella visited him and he painted her portrait; in mid-August he was in Brussels.

While working at the Luxembourg paintings, Rubens had painted, in 1624, a composition commissioned twelve years previously: *The Conversion of St Bavon*, for the church consecrated to the saint at Ghent. The vicissitudes of this painting give an idea of the disagreeable conditions in which he often had to work *(Pl. 85)*.

84 *Portrait of the Duke of Buckingham, c.* 1625

Finally it was Bishop Antoine Triest, a great patron, who decided that the work should be painted, and had a pompous architectural construction built as a setting for it. This was replaced between 1702-19 by another, the work of the Antwerp sculptor Pierre Verbruggen, and removed to the Church of St-Gommaire at Lier, while Rubens' picture was relegated to a chapel in the ambulatory.

It is a superb piece of bravura in high-flown Baroque style, consisting of two scenes, one above the other, linked by a staircase. Above, Count Alowin de la Hesbaye, the future St Bavon, renouncing his warlike and dissipated life, is arriving at the convent, on whose threshold St Amand and the Abbé Florbert greet him. Below, Rubens shows what he has left behind: his wife, surrounded by her female companions, bewails his departure, while a steward distributes her wealth to the poor. The superimposition of the scenes is composed by two parallel movements rising from right to left on both sides of the staircase, and accented above by the upward movement of the future saint, on one knee before the prelates who greet him, and below by the turning movement of the beggars, rolling and unrolling round the figure of the steward.

The sketch submitted in 1612 to the Bishop Charles Maes belongs to the National Gallery, and it shows that at first Rubens intended a triptych. Max Rooses[60] claims that in the 1624 painting the upper figures were painted by a pupil and retouched by Rubens; but a simple examination proves this to be wrong. The figures are painted with the scumble technique and swift strokes which are typical of Rubens' work of this period.

The *Adoration of the Magi* for the high altar of St-Michel in Antwerp was also painted in 1624, and tradition has it that the great Fleming finished it in thirteen days. Even if this is inaccurate—the canvas is almost 4 × 50 m. high, and more than 3 m. wide—such a story bears witness to Rubens' swiftness of execution, which his contemporaries so much admired. Today this huge painting, by his hand alone, is in the Royal Museum in Antwerp. The painter received 1,500 florins, in two payments. Since the first was paid on 23 December 1624, the painting must have been delivered, as was customary, a little before that date. The sketch is in the Wallace Collection.

Against a theatrical yet worldly scene Rubens has placed an imposing succession of figures; statuesque, yet carried on a powerful Baroque swell, in heavy, opulent material and dramatic poses, as if carved in stone by a Bernini. Irresistibly they invade the painting, where the master has once again demonstrated his power to loose and bind the forces which inhabit it. A wide and moving curve begins at the top

85   *The Conversion of St Bavon,* 1624

with the Nubian camel-drivers perched on their animals, and passes through the central group to arrive finally at the delightful figures of Mary and her child.

Not all the characters have their eyes fixed on the newborn Child; on the contrary, their looks diverge. If a series of lines were to be drawn from their eyes, veiled with tenderness or staring wide, these would enclose the composition like a network corresponding to the distribution of masses. The basis of the composition is a pyramid balanced by a median vertical axis. The colour is warm, glowing, Venetian, and it adds fire to the robust rhetoric of the work. The brush has attacked the whole at one blow; mounting from the shadows to the lights, it has given to all the forms, masses and colours the trembling vitality of a river in flood.

86   *Lot's Flight*, 1625

87   *Lot and his Daughters*

Lot's Flight (Pl. 86), signed and dated 1625, was in Richelieu's collection before it went to the Louvre, but it is not known whether he commissioned it or merely acquired it. Its dissonance of colour does not affect the sculptural grandeur of the forms with their broad rhythms. A few years previously, probably about 1620, the artist had represented the same subject in another painting, now in the Martin von Wagner Museum in the University of Würzburg.

The negotiations and discussions in which Rubens took part do not seem to have affected his activity as a painter. At forty-five his strength seemed undiminished; he organized his life and all its demands, which he met with enthusiasm, in such a way as to bring all he did to a successful conclusion. This suggests an exceptional character, great self-knowledge and a strong will.

CHAPTER EIGHT

Diplomat and artist

While Rubens pursued his copious political activities Isabella Brandt brought up their children in the fine house in the Wapperstraat, to which her husband continually added fine things: objects and paintings brought back from his travels. Among the pictures were Titians, Tintorettos, Van Eycks, Holbeins, Bronzinos and Correggios; as well as works by his friends Brouwer (eighteen of whose canvases he possessed), Snyders, Wildens, Jan Brueghel, Van Dyck, Josse de Momper, Paul de Vos and Pieter Seghers. There were also drawings by Dürer, Veronese, Titian, Tintoretto, and others.

The house had a welcome for everyone. The year before Isabella's death Golnitzius of Danzig, secretary to King Christian IV of Denmark, spoke with enthusiasm of the artistic riches amassed by the great painter, saying that his pen was incapable of describing all the sculptures, goldsmith's work and pictures. It is not surprising that many prominent persons should have come to see these collections.

Was it a premonition which caused Rubens at this time (1625-26) to wish to paint his beloved wife *(Pl. 89)*? Two portraits of Isabella, aged thirty-four, date from these years: the somewhat stiff one in the Uffizi, which seems rather an official picture than an intimate essay, and the truer and more expressive portrait in the Cleveland Museum of Art, which reflects the melancholy of this resigned being, who lived in the shadow and took no part in her husband's brilliant career. Our knowledge of their relations would be greater had not Rubens' private correspondence been lost.

She had, admittedly, three children, and a large household to look after. Little Clara-Serena's death, and then her own illness— probably tuberculosis— which was to prove fatal, both darkened her existence. Rapidly but observantly, with the light touch which was peculiar to him, Rubens caresses the face he loved with soft, rich colours which add to the brilliance of her curiously fixed gaze.

Rubens' portraits are animated by the flesh rather than by the spirit, and it is not astonishing that Isabella, the little bourgeoise, whose character was not striking, but who was pious and modest, should have failed to inspire him. He shows more enthusiasm and more verve with the resplendent Hélène Fourment, whom he seems to appreciate like some succulent fruit. The models of Rubens who seem most alive arouse no curiosity as to what they may think or say; they are present bodily rather than mentally. The Magi, the Apostles, the philosophers and martyrs, are a different matter; in their visionary eyes their souls show through and Rubens' psychology is seen to be powerful. Its strength lies in the similarity of his interior life to theirs.

Isabella Brandt died on 20 June 1626, aged thirty-five. She left her husband helpless. He contemplated, in the great empty house, giving up painting. This, at any rate, is what he says, though his responsibilities, his commissions and his Regent all opposed the idea as impossible. On 15 July he wrote[61] to Pierre Dupuy:

'As for myself, I have lost a very pleasant companion, whom I could and must in reason love; for she had none of the faults of her sex. She was neither morose-tempered nor weak; but so kind, so good and so virtuous that everyone loved her during her life, and mourns her since her death. Such a loss touches my inmost being; and since the only cure for all our ills is forgetfulness, child of time, I must needs await from him my only comfort. But it will be hard for me to disentangle my sorrow from the memory I shall hold all my life of this dear and adored soul.

'I believe that travel would help, for it would tear me away from the sight of all that surrounds me, and at length revive me from my misery...'

88   *Self-Portrait*   89   *Isabella Brandt, c.* 1625

The political situation and international events served to distract him, and his frequent letters to Dupuy show the interest he continued to take in them. In November he spent three weeks in Paris, where he met a number of his friends, and at the beginning of December he was at Calais with the works of art he had sold to the Duke of Buckingham. In Brussels, where he ceased his travels, he felt the first twinges of the gout or rheumatism which was to plague him incessantly and finally carry him off fourteen years later.

He would soon be fifty. Most of his greatest works had been painted and he was at the pinnacle of his glory. Two successive bereavements had clouded his life; otherwise it was of a brightness difficult to imagine in the tangled Europe of Richelieu, Charles I and Philip IV.

His dignity, resilience and tact were remarkable, and his love of intrigue never drew him into circles where espionage mingled with crime. He had desired a title, and the King of Spain and his Regent had readily granted it. They and others among his contemporaries had praised his handling of diplomatic affairs, to which his knowledge, eloquence and elegance all contributed.

Today the painter's world is unlimited. Rubens was known and admired by a few thousand persons only; but he carried in his head the whole of his world: the monarchist and Catholic Occident whose champion he was, and by whose scale he deserves to be measured, artistically and politically. If he was confident about the world of his imagination—and his painting shows it—he was anxious, and with reason, about the less stable world of men in which he lived. His dream was of peace; and it was not to be realized. Renouncing it, he would return to the world of his art; face to face, that is to say, with the idea of perfection.

It is a mistake to try to isolate Rubens from his time, especially since his time understood and appreciated him in both his roles. Because two worlds encountered in him, he could speak to all men. 'I hold,' he once wrote, 'the whole world to be my country.' He was now entering upon the dazzling maturity of his existence.

The art of engraving was already flourishing in Antwerp when Rubens, shortly after his return from Italy, decided to found a studio for the reproduction of his paintings. Unfortunately the artists he employed could not carry out his wishes, and he got rid of them after one or two unhappy attempts.

In 1620 he became acquainted with Lucas Vorsterman, Dutch by origin, who worked for two years in a studio adjacent to Rubens' in the Wapperstraat. He left owing to a quarrel, after having reproduced a large number of the painter's works, whose style he managed to translate to copper in a masterly fashion. There was no one in Antwerp for years afterwards to equal Vorsterman, who, after a visit to England, returned to work with Van Dyck from 1630 onwards.

Rubens had thus to content himself with less sensitive, though capable, men, such as Paul Pontius, Boëtius a Bolswert, Schelte a Bolswert, and Christopher Jegher, who was the only one who engraved on wood.

Jegher had worked at the Plantin printing works as a carver in wood. This was the main intellectual centre of Antwerp after the town was recaptured by the Spanish in 1585. Printers who had been associated with reform had to fly to Holland to escape prison or the stake, and there they became the creators of the young republic's prosperity, to the detriment of their native town. Their numbers were sufficient to cause the decay of the printing industry in Antwerp, to which the Spaniards gave a new lease of life by publishing large numbers of theological and devotional works. Christoph Plantin, nicknamed in spite of himself 'the King's Arch-typographer', enjoyed a monopoly of this trade in Spain and her colonies. This was the beginning of his fortune, and enabled him to become the prototype

90   *Christoph Plantin*   91   *J. Rivière, wife of Plantin*

of the modern publisher of the industrial era: in thirty-three years over 1,500 titles were produced on his presses *(Pl. 90)*.

Plantin's son-in-law, Jan Moretus, succeeded him at his death, and it was with him that Rubens, whose first work as an illustrator had been done in 1608, started to work. In 1612 the painter became the Plantin press' official designer. His childhood friend Balthazar Moretus had just taken over. Their association was continuous until 1637, when it became intermittent owing to the decline in Rubens' health. He then limited himself to directing others, and to 'inventing', in the contemporary phrase, drawings carried out by the painter Quellin, who did not so much collaborate with, as receive orders from the master.

The first of Moretus' publications illustrated by Rubens was the *Opticorum Libri Sex* of Aquilonius (1613). He executed for it a frontispiece and six vignettes. For the *Missale Romanum* he designed a Calvary; and for the new edition of the *Brevarium Romanum* which appeared in the same year (1614), a frontispiece and ten figures, part of which was reproduced in the *Missale*. In the following year Rubens ornamented his brother's posthumous work *S. Asterii Amasae Homiliae* with a portrait of the saint; for Seneca's *Opera* he engraved an effigy of Justus Lipsius, a bust of the author, and the traditional scene representing the philosopher dying in his bath. Henceforth he drew only two more portraits—of the Jesuit Father Leonard Lessius, and of Urban VIII, for the *Opuscula* of the first and the *Poemata* of the second—limiting himself to frontispieces *(Pl. 92)*. It would take too long to list all the works[62] for which Rubens conceived drawings, engraved mostly by Corneille Galle, a master of technique whom Rubens admired. His brother Theodor Galle, Lucas Vorsterman the great 'translator' of his paintings, and Charles de Mallery also worked for Rubens until Erasmus Quellin began to compose frontispieces according to Rubens' indications. In 1638 that of the *Equisitis Legatus* by François de Marselaer was the only one by Rubens' own hand. The work

FRANCISCI HARÆI

ANNALES

DVCVM SEV PRINCIPVM

BRABANTIÆ

TOTIVSQ. BELGII.

TOMI TRES:
Quorum Primo solius Brabantiæ,
Secundo Belgii vniti Principvm
res gestæ; Tertio Belgici tvmvltvs,
vsque ad Indvcias anno M. DC. IX.
pactas, enarrantur.

Cum Dvcvm seu Principvm Imaginibus,
et breui rerum per omnem Evropam
illustrium narratione.

ANTVERPIÆ,
EX OFFICINA PLANTINIANA
Apud Balthasarem Moretum
et Viduam Ioannis Moreti
et Io. Meursium.
M. DC. XXIII.

92 *Frontispiece of 'Annals ducum seu principun Brabantiae'* (Haraens), 1623

93　*Adoration of the Magi, c.* 1618

did not, however, appear until 1666. The wood engravings for the
Roman Missal by Christoph Jegher after Rubens' own drawings
remain the only illustrations after Rubens in this medium (1625-27).

The painter of the *Raising of the Cross* conceived his frontispieces
more as a humanist than as a painter. The works they embellished
were learned and philosophical ones, and they were composed in
this spirit, furnished with allegorical elements and symbols which
Rubens often amused himself, as was traditional, by making into
actual rebuses whose solution would be supplied by the publisher
in a note. Classical balance and a decorative appearance characterize
these compositions, which tried to express the author's ideas, or

at least his intentions. Later examples are freer in execution, and have in them more of the Baroque; but they are always in the spirit proper to their kind. Still later they become calmer once more; gravity gains on expressionism; but they become academic only under the hand of the less gifted, more painstaking Quellin.

Naturally Rubens' frontispiece drawings are far less accomplished than his studies for paintings; the line did not excite him, and drawing is less important in his work than colour and mass, through which above all he expressed himself. The drawings were done quickly, probably at odd moments, and are not always free—probably for this reason—from carelessness and heaviness; but they were sufficient for their purpose.

Rubens was not a painter who felt that there were certain humbler areas of art which were beneath him. He was ready for all experiments and techniques. He supplied the sketch for the statue of St Norbert which his friend Hans van Mildert modelled for the high altar of the abbey of St-Michel. He drew designs for ivory statuettes carved by Jörg Petel, Van Opstal and Luc Fay d'Herbe who most probably worked under Rubens' direction on the sculptures which decorated his house. He also designed goldsmith's and silversmith's work, including a silver basin for Charles I, modelled by Theodor Rogiers, and his book illustrations and cartoons for tapestries such as *The Story of Decius Mus*, *The Life of Constantine* and the *Triumph of the Eucharist* have already been touched upon.

Thanks to the prudent policies of the Archduke and his wife Isabella, the Spanish occupation of Flanders was milder in character than it had once been; but the severity of the repression was not forgotten. The Church kept a close watch on morals, and tended towards fanaticism and the encouragement of manifestations in which flagellation and convulsions did their best to arouse the zeal of a somewhat unresponsive population. Non-Catholics were outlawed, and had to become converted or leave the country. To miss the Mass on two out of three Sundays could entail excommunication;

and there were powerful Spaniards who would have welcomed a return of the fires in which so many heretics had already expired.

In this once free and happy country the spirit of inquiry was dead; intellectual energies were now devoted to religious propaganda. The Flemish taste for spectacle remained, but the spectacles had undergone an unhappy change. Secular festivities had given place to religious processions; gambling and procuring had been driven underground; and ostentation and display, freedom and familiarity, had succumbed to secrecy and hypocrisy.

The Church in Flanders, following the example of that of Spain, covered itself with black robes and ashes. Nocturnal offices and funeral obsequies were multiplied; ceremonies of expiation were invented; processions representing the Passion appeared at the height of August; suffering was exalted and the spectre of sin was everywhere. Calvaries and Pietàs rose at street crossings, and innocent distractions were replaced by gloomy ones, commemorative services, sermons. Not a day passed but the Carmelites or Jesuits, the Recollects, Minims or Franciscans, discovered an ascetic to celebrate as an example, or a saint to pray to.

Only painters appeared to have the courage to extol in their pictures, under the pretext of myth or allegory, the charms of the women of Flanders. Rubens certainly did not restrain himself in defying the sanctimonious in this fashion. His Madonnas are as generous as one could wish, with their pretty faces, tender smiles, and round bosoms. His nudes display their charms without shame. But there is no eroticism here: only an expression of the last freedom retained by the Flemish. At most, this is the healthy sensuousness of a man from whom pretty women held few secrets. Alone, or almost alone, among his contemporaries, Rubens refused to discriminate between religious and secular painting, or to give up an imagery which was now frowned upon. He was, notwithstanding, a zealous supporter of the new spirit which saw art as a means of defending the Church against Protestantism. In his eyes the defence

94 *Triumph of the Church*, 1627

of the Roman faith and of the future of western civilization was of the highest importance and worth all his efforts both as painter and diplomat. His Christian feelings inspired him in his work and were his source of equilibrium as a person, just as religion itself fed the idea of the universal harmony which was his ultimate dream.   If he, the exile's son, whose country had been occupied, ravaged and mutilated by the Spanish soldiery, and suffocated by their priests, had become the tireless and devoted servant and champion of Spain, it was because Spain was in his eyes the solid bastion of Christianity.

Wherever the forces of Philip IV and Charles I met, those of the English King suffered; besides, there was growing discontent against the disastrous anti-Spanish policy of Buckingham. On the signing of the Treaty of Monzon between Spain and France (15 March 1626), Charles I found himself isolated in the face of a European coalition, and Buckingham at once decided to send a secret emissary to Madrid to try to put an end to hostilities.

Rubens can hardly have had an opportunity to see the Duke again. It has been suggested that Buckingham may have seen him in Antwerp in December 1625 on the occasion of his visit to the Hague to sign the treaty with Holland; but this is unlikely since England and Spain were at war at the time. Rubens' relations with the Duke were now carried on through Gerbier, with whom he corresponded continuously, though distrusting him as a wily practitioner of clandestine diplomacy. As for Gerbier, he proceeded all the more cautiously since he suspected that Buckingham's fall from power was approaching.

In January 1627 Gerbier asked Rubens to procure a passport for him so that he might come to Brussels to present to Isabella

95   *Triumph of the Eucharist*, 1627

an important proposal from the Duke. He arrived a month later. The proposal was for an armistice with Spain and a free trade pact between Spain, England, Denmark and the United Provinces.

The Infanta replied that she preferred to limit this pact to England and Spain alone. Charles I accepted. Madrid may have been hoping that he would refuse, especially since the Franco-Spanish treaty envisaged the conquest of England in order to re-establish Catholicism in that country. In order to avoid any trouble with Richelieu, therefore, the preliminary negotiations were back-dated fifteen months—to before the Treaty of Monzon, in fact.

It was probably at the beginning of 1627 that Isabella commissioned from Rubens the eighteen cartoons for tapestries illustrating the *Triumph of the Eucharist* for the Convent of Discalced Carmelites of Madrid, where the cartoons still are. The painter made, as usual, sketches for submission to the interested parties; he then completed the 'patterns' for the tapestry weavers. The tapestries represent the Catholic dogma of the Real Presence—a principal cause of contention between them and the Protestants. They were thus not only works to the glory of the Counter-Reformation, but weapons against heresy, which Rubens regarded as the source of the worst disorders of society *(Pl. 95)*.

Many versions of the various sketches and cartoons are extant. The cartoons, having been used by the Brussels weavers, were kept in the Governor-General's palace, and then, in 1648, sent on Philip IV's orders to Madrid. Six of them were later presented to the church in Loches, not far from Madrid, but they were removed by French troops during Napoleon's campaigns. Two of them, belonging to the Louvre, are at present in the Museum of Valenciennes, and the other four belonged to the Duke of Westminster before being acquired by the Ringling Museum in Sarasota, Florida. These 'patterns', painted with the artist's usual virtuosity, are conceived in a grandiose decorative style, and peopled with numerous figures whose noble gestures correspond with the amplitude of the composi-

96 *Philip IV wearing the chain of the Order of the Golden Fleece*

tions, which are full and free from superfluous spaces. They or the copies made from them were used to weave several series of tapestries, among them those in the National Palace, Madrid; the Imperial Collections, Vienna; Toledo Cathedral; the Schnütgen Museum, Cologne; and various private collections.

Rubens' travels, discussions and negotiations were filled alternatively with hope and disillusion. Madrid was against all peaceful schemes, and the Duke of Olivarez, the real master of Spain, declared that the rebel provinces would be subdued by arms alone. France, on the other hand, although Philip IV's ally, gave its support to the States-General. This further complicated an already confused situation, whose details emerge in Rubens' letters to Pierre Dupuy, to Gerbier and, through Gerbier, to the Duke of Buckingham himself.

Rubens' insistence on obtaining peace surprised Philip IV, who had never got rid of a certain mistrust of the diplomat-cum-artist. Wishing to see for himself what Rubens' intentions were, he asked in June 1628 that all the painter's correspondence relative to the negotiations should be sent him. Rubens accepted, but asked to be allowed to accompany the documents himself. His request was granted. He left Antwerp in the strictest secrecy during the last days of August. On 23 August Buckingham was assassinated at Portsmouth.

The explanations which Rubens, documents in hand, delivered to the Junta were unanimously approved, and Philip IV saw to it that they were pursued. For the artist this was a 'satisfecit' of which he could justly be proud. Its sequel was even more flattering. The King placed at his disposal a studio, in his own palace, and commanded him to paint not only his own portrait but, at the request of the Infanta, those of all the members of the royal family. Rubens lost no time in telling Peiresc the news. Pacheco, Velazquez's father-in-law, reports that Rubens painted five portraits of the King, one of them an equestrian portrait. This one, which is mentioned in the 1636 inventory of the royal collections in Madrid, was certainly destroyed in the fire at the palace in 1734. Possibly the version in the Uffizi, painted, as it is believed, by Carreño, is a copy of it. L. Burchard and R. A. d'Hulst[63] are of the opinion that the bust portrait of Philip IV belonging to the Kunsthaus, Zurich, is the prototype of all the various versions painted partly or wholly by Rubens and by portrait specialists among his collaborators *(Pl. 96)*.

Those of Elizabeth of Bourbon are of equally variable character. Philip IV's wife, who was reckoned one of the beauties of her time, hated sitting; and Rubens therefore limited himself to one portrait, of her face only (Kunsthistorisches Museum, Vienna).

While in Madrid the Fleming made a number of copies, or rather interpretations, of works by the painter he most admired: Titian The complete list includes twenty-one canvases after Titian, nine after Raphael and one after Tintoretto. Besides the numerous portraits which claimed his attention (Charles V, Cardinal Ippolito de' Medici, Duke Alba, the Doge Gritti, the Emperor Ferdinand, Isabella d'Este, etc.), should be mentioned *The Bacchanal*, to which Rubens gave increased fluidity by means of a luminosity which unifies its masses; *Adam and Eve in Paradise; Adonis and Venus*, etc. Pacheco, in *El Arte de la Pintura*[64], gives a list of the copies made from paintings in the possession of Philip IV.

It has been said that Rubens' motive for painting this large number of copies in Madrid was to disguise the real reasons for his visit. This is possible; but his attachment to the great Italian is undoubted. He admired his vigorous imagination, his generous forms, his sense of mass and volume, the fullness of his colouring and light, and the sensuousness which at his best animates and transfigures the faces of his women. It is of Titian that Rubens must have talked most often with one of the few artists in Madrid he became friendly with: Diego de Velazquez, then aged twenty-nine. The contrast between the little, spare *hidalgo* dressed in black and the dazzling ambassador-painter must have been extraordinary. Of their conver-

97 *Hector killed by Achilles*

sations we know little or nothing; but it is clear that the differences between them were not confined to their respective ages: they included their origins, societies, outlooks and styles. Velazquez was discreet, sober, moderate; Rubens overbearing, explosive, fertile. Velazquez was anxious for discoveries, Rubens surfeited with knowledge.

On 24 April 1629, France and England decided to conclude the peace, which was signed on 16 September following. On 13 May Rubens was back from Spain and at Brussels. Philip IV had loaded

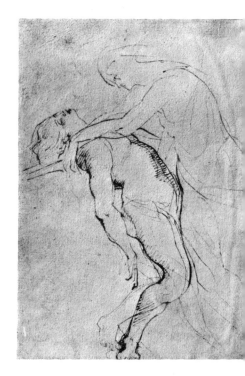

98   *Portrait of Titian*   99   *The Death of Adonis*

him with presents and honours, and then—a mark of unusual favour—decided to send him to London pending the exchange of accredited ambassadors for the signing of the peace. Although the post was a temporary one Rubens was satisfied; he was now the recognized representative of His Catholic Majesty, and therefore had all the means he needed to achieve his objective: the return of the seceded provinces. On 5 June he arrived in the English capital, and Charles I received him at Greenwich.

His stay in London was not a happy one. A new French ambassador, Chateauneuf, had arrived to work against the Anglo-Spanish *rapprochement*. Richelieu, reverting to Henri IV's policy, was trying to destroy one by one the powers surrounding France, particularly Spain and Habsburg Austria. While Chateauneuf pressed the English to join fleets with the Dutch and infest the coasts of Spain, a powerful faction was pushing the King to cancel his agreement with the French. Rubens, anxious, and on top of that racked with rheumatism, pressed Madrid incessantly to sign with London a treaty which would put an end to this dangerous situation. Even the receptions and banquets in his honour failed to distract him from his anxiety.

Charles I commissioned him to paint an *Allegory of Peace and War (Pl. 101)*—a suitable theme for the times—and a conventional *St George and the Dragon*. He painted a further portrait of his friend the Earl of Arundel, and had as another sitter a certain 'Old Parr' who was chiefly remarkable for being, reputedly, 142 years old. But Rubens left no more masterpieces in London than he had in Madrid.

The business dragged on. The court awaited, somewhat ironically, the arrival of Philip IV's official ambassador to replace the 'semi-official' Rubens, whose promotion was looked at askance by the career diplomats. But Don Carlos Coloma seemed in no hurry to leave Madrid, though his English counterpart Sir Francis Cottington was already on his way there. Chateauneuf, seeing this threat to an agreement between England and Spain, was jubilant. Rubens, tired of the intrigue of the court, wished only to return to Antwerp to paint.

At last Coloma arrived, on 7 January 1630, after six months' delay. Olivarez insisted that Rubens remain in London until the agreement was signed. He sighed and resigned himself—fortunately, as it turned out, for Charles I, like Philip IV, heaped on him honours, titles and presents.

Eventually he arrived back in Brussels for the traditional 'report' to Isabella, who confirmed the King of Spain's decision and appointed him Secretary to the Privy Council of the Netherlands. The post was a sinecure and could pass on to his son in the event of his death or resignation. On 6 April 1630 he was once again in Antwerp.

The question now arose whether he should undertake the second gallery for the Luxembourg Palace, in honour of Henri IV. Surprisingly, considering that his political activity leading to the Anglo-Spanish agreement had made him Richelieu's enemy, he still thought that this work might be completed. Pretending ignorance of the real reasons why he had lost his 'fortune in France', as he wrote to Pierre Dupuy[65], he piously deplored 'some misunderstanding as to the dimensions and symmetry of this gallery in honour of *Henri le Grand*', adding: 'I have said, in general terms, that to meet with so many difficulties at the commencement of this undertaking seems to me inauspicious, for I am deprived of courage and, to speak truthfully, somewhat disgusted by the innovations and changes to my own prejudice and that of the work itself, whose splendours and lustre will be greatly diminished by these retrenchments...' The 'difficulties' mainly concern 'the King's triumph at the end of the gallery', which Rubens had begun, but which was never finished. It is called *The Triumphal Entry of Henri IV into Paris*, freely inspired by Mantegna's *Triumph of Caesar* which Rubens had seen in Mantua.

100   *Tournament beside a Castle Moat, c.* 1638

101 *Allegory of Peace and War, c. 1630*

But it seems extraordinary that Rubens was unaware that this was a lost cause, or that he hoped to outmanoeuvre Richelieu.

Six more compositions remained unfinished, and are listed in the inventory of Rubens' studio as 'Six large pieces, unfinished, including sieges of towns, battles and triumphs of Henri Fourth, King of France, which were begun some years since for the gallery of the Luxembourg hotel of the Queen Mother of France.' Two of them are lost. *The Battle of Ivry* and *Triumphal Entry (Pl. 102)* are in the Uffizi; *Henri IV at the Battle of St-Martin-l'Eglise* is in the Pinakothek, Munich; *Henri IV in Battle* belongs to the August Nuerburg

The Triumphal Entry of Henri IV into Paris after the Battle of Ivry

collection in Hamburg. A preliminary version of *The Entry of Henri IV* is in the Wallace Collection, and there are monochrome sketches in private collections and at the Metropolitan Museum. A sketch for a painting not in fact carried out, *Henri IV receiving the Sceptre from his People*, belongs to a collection in Munich. The Musée Bonnat, Bayonne, possesses sketches of *The Battle of Ivry* and *The Entry into Paris*.

The Uffizi and Munich paintings show the painter's extraordinary swiftness of execution, and an ease of invention equal to that of *La Vie de Marie de Médicis;* they make the abandonment of the second Luxembourg gallery seem all the more regrettable. On 27 March 1631 Rubens, having by now abandoned all hope, wrote to Pierre Dupuy that he was giving up work on *La Vie de Henri IV* owing to an accumulation of difficulties and delays.

Even so, he could hardly complain about the French court's treatment of him. Louis XIII had, after all, commissioned him in

103 *Albert and Nicolas Rubens, c.* 1625

1622 to carry out a series of twelve designs for tapestries representing *The Life of Constantine*. The sketches, rapidly executed, since Peiresc saw four of them in Paris in November of the same year, attracted some criticism; on the other hand the exactness of the Roman costumes was unanimously praised by 'those men whom the King charged,' as Peiresc wrote, 'with the inspection of public works.' The painter answered these observations with good grace, but his interest in the fate of the academic *Life of Constantine* was obviously slight.

The tapestries, woven at the Gobelins establishment from Rubens' designs belong to the Mobilier National of France. Certain pieces have been placed in the Châteaux of Blois and Azay-le-Rideau.

CHAPTER NINE

The celebration of flesh and spirit

On 6 December 1630 Rubens married, at the Church of St-Jacques in Antwerp, Hélène, the youngest of his friend Daniel Fourment's eleven children. He was fifty-three years old; she was sixteen. His eccentric action carried his painting to its sublimest heights, and added to the work of this champion of the monarchy and the Church a marvellous chapter in celebration of the flesh.

Hélène was utterly intoxicating physically: pink, white and splendidly endowed. She was Rubens' ideal, and strikingly similar in appearance to Isabella. She bore him five children: Claire-Jeanne (baptized 18 January 1632); François (12 July 1633); Isabella-Hélène (3 May 1635); and Peter Paul (1 April 1639). Constance-Albertine, born posthumously, was baptized on 3 February 1641, nine months after the painter's death.

Thus a new queen entered the kingdom. Hélène moved into the house in the Wapperstraat, which she knew from her visits with her parents, feeling a little intimidated at the thought of being the mistress of so many beautiful things. A little shy, too, since it was a kind of fairy-tale.

Rubens was helplessly and hopelessly in love with her. He ignored the spiteful talk about his gluttonous pursuit of young flesh and the identical ages of his eldest son and his new wife. He knew that with Hélène, as with Isabella before her, he would have a freedom and autonomy which would not have been possible with the well-born or rich elder ladies of Antwerp who were more eligible.

In the matter of love he had everything to teach her; and, attacks of rheumatism apart, there were blissful moments, the ritual of

104 *Rubens, his Wife and Son Nicolas in their garden*, 1631

toilette not excepted. He was so happy with his child-wife and so proud of her beauty that he showed her off to everyone. With complete absence of shame he left no one in doubt of her charms. In the eyes of the whole world, and for all time, the Venus of the Wapperstraat threw wide open the doors of her bedroom or bathroom and displayed her nakedness. Rubens stood at the threshold. 'She is his goddess,' wrote Roger Avermaete, 'and he presents her as goddess to the world.' So much for the hypocrites and the bigots! But no one protested; his standing was too great. Even the Church was silent.

The works painted before Isabella's death are calm, well-balanced, serene. After *La Vie de Marie de Médicis*, the grand organ of his art, excepting always the splendid Baroque tumult of the *Adoration of the Magi*, becomes attenuated in tone. The official portraits are cold and conventional, and the cartoons for the *Triumph of the Eucharist* and *The Life of Constantine* are even a little academic. The paintings he had done in Madrid and London added little to his glory; the period of exaltation seemed past. On the other hand he had been preoccupied by politics, and deplored the fact that painting had become only an occasional pursuit.

Age too had brought peacefulness; and his grief at Isabella's death, and the emptiness it left behind both contributed to the lassitude which now seemed to invade his stormy genius. Henceforward one could expect in his work more nobility and less petulance, more greatness and reflectiveness and less instinct and emotion.

But a girl of sixteen was to upset all that. Her beauty was to unloose a storm whose violence no one could have foreseen. It is possible that she contributed to the shortening of her elderly husband's life; but his ten years with her transformed his work into a sensuous poem in which his genius unfolded in triumphant happiness.

He felt the need now to be free and to proclaim his freedom. No more constraints, prejudices, obstacles: he wanted to live. Looking at the Titians in Madrid, he had seen that life was made up of light and colour and youth and love. They now entered his own existence and his own painting. Isabella's aloofness had presided over the great Baroque decorative works, and he had lent her face to his Virgins. Hélène's face he would also give them; but he gave it as well to Venus, Andromeda and Diana; to jolly peasant girls, and to nymphs at bacchanals. The lovely courtesans of the *Garden of Love* are themselves the adored mistress, ten times repeated, of the old lover who still felt the spur of the senses and who put his ecstasies as well as his regrets into his paintings.

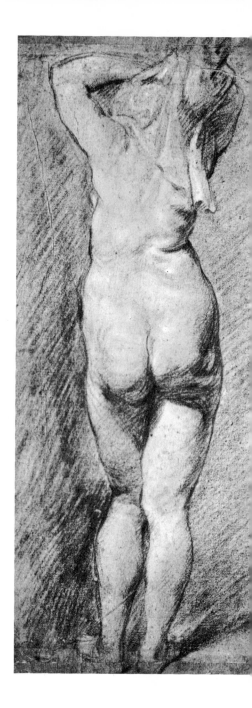

105 *Nude standing Man, with
drapery floating from his shoulder*

106 *Nude Woman from behind*

107 *Hélène Fourment in
a Fur Coat, c.* 1631

On 15 December 1630, a few days after the wedding, the treaty between England and Spain was at last signed. But Rubens' goal —peace with Holland, and the union of the seventeen provinces— was still a long way off. Nor were the States-General and the court of Madrid helping matters.

On 21 December, Olivarez suggested nominating Rubens as the Spanish Ambassador to England. The Junta received this proposal with disfavour, owing to Rubens' commitments as a painter, as it explained. The 'specialists' succeeded in getting Jean de Necolalde appointed. Rubens was suggested as a replacement for him until he was able to travel to the English capital. But this time it was Rubens who refused. If he were not chosen as ambassador, he would not go as a stop-gap. This incident shows that, in spite of all his resolutions, and of the fever of creative activity in which he now found himself, Rubens was still willing, under certain conditions, to abandon painting for politics; and this seems a remarkable thing.

In love, and happily so, Rubens still remained his own master. His style grew broader, and expressed a new delight in colour: yellows, ultramarines, vermilions, crimsons reigned where before had been ochres, browns, blues and greens. Half-tints expressed modulations, but earth-tones had disappeared: colours sang in the shadows as in the light. And the light spread like caresses: here insistent, there light and rapid, nourished by crimsons and bright reds, and expressing the joy of life as the best of Rubens' inheritors were to express it: Fragonard, Delacroix, Renoir. Glow of dawn; brightness of noon; gold of evening: Rubens more than ever looked at nature. In his own house too, where the body of Hélène reflected the light again.

It is difficult to assign dates to the portraits of his wife: alone or with her children; nude, half-dressed or sumptuously bedecked; in bridal dress or in court costume, covered with jewels and deeply décolletée. Her form grew more majestic with time, but lost nothing of its firmness.

One morning, leaving her bath, she catches his eye with something like a shock. He throws her fur-lined pelisse round her and paints her. Heavier than before she had children, her skin is still pearly, steeped in light, and tinged with rose. Her fair hair tied with a bandeau, she looks with intelligent, amused eyes out of a pink face, a little surprised, as if she wonders why her husband insists on painting her all the time *(Pl. 107)*.

This painting, which the artist kept jealously in his studio, is today in the Kunsthistorisches Museum, Vienna. It is not the portrait of a soul. It expresses no interior life, and says nothing of Hélène's character. She is the incarnation of the adage: 'Be beautiful: be silent.' No doubt she was a good wife, mother, manager; but she was above all a good model and a good mistress.

The best-known portrait of Hélène Fourment is in the Louvre. Judging by the apparent ages of the children, Rubens must have painted it about 1636-37. Its treatment is that of a sketch, and its lightness and dexterity recall the 'fa presto' of the Venetian Baroque painters, whose colouring—pearly, with the yellows heightened by crimsons or vermilions, pinks or golden greys—it also shares. Probably Rubens intended to expand this sketch into a finished composition, as he had often done *(Pl. 108)*.

Hélène, who has now become heavier, seems to be looking tenderly and a little anxiously at her son François seated on her knees. Her daughter Claire-Jeanne, their eldest child, stands in front of her. On the right, merely indicated, a baby's hand holds the chair. It belongs almost certainly to Isabella-Hélène, born in 1635.

The work, though unfinished and in some places only touched, is, a miracle. Almost monochromatic, and at once realistic and poetic, it is a declaration of love to Hélène; and, through her, to youth and life itself. One guesses with what tenderness this bouquet of joy was painted. Its transparencies are amber and tortoiseshell; its sweetness is full of juice; it is clothed in gold and flows with honey. The comparison with his portrait, twenty years earlier, of Isabella

108   *Hélène Fourment and her Children, c. 1636*

and himself, is eloquent; it shows the distance travelled between the traditional composition of bourgeois Flanders and the freedom of style of European Baroque, which carries all before it and makes beauty even from what is facile and negligent in it.

The finest portraits of Hélène Fourment, apart from the admirable trio of the Louvre and the one in Vienna, are those in Munich, in one of which she is shown in gorgeous wedding attire, and in the other with her son on her knees *(Pl. 112)*. A magnificent bust portrait, belonging to Baron Edouard de Rothschild, shows her dressed in black, wearing a mantilla which she holds aside with her hand. It is painted opulently and generously. No less fine is the portrait in the Robert Finck Collection in Brussels: full-fleshed and tender, its handling, like that of the Louvre painting, betrays the painter's emotion.

Rubens had taken his wife to Brussels and presented her to his Regent, who had smiled affably from under her Poor Clare's hood at the girl whose husband had dressed her up for the occasion like a reliquary-shrine. Back then to Antwerp in his coach: he had sat down at his easel to take up the work which politics had interrupted. He would show his wife to all Antwerp. Nevertheless peace was not concluded, and the union of the seventeen provinces seemed more and more uncertain—even perhaps illusory.

In Paris, Marie de Médicis was once more in revolt, this time against her former protégé Richelieu, now absolute master of France. As had happened before, her plot had failed and she had had to fly. Hemmed in by the Cardinal's troops, she saw as her only refuge some foreign country. Surely the good and pious Isabella would not refuse her? Isabella did in fact consent. And who should be chosen as the diplomat and counsellor to arrange the Queen Mother's move to Brussels, but Rubens? His relations with her through the Luxembourg paintings, and his experience in such matters, made him the obvious choice. He himself was delighted at the prospect: he could even score off Richelieu.

On 26 July 1631 he was appointed as the Infanta's representative in her dealings with Marie de Médicis. On the evening of 12 August, Marie entered Brussels amid general rejoicing. In mid-September she visited Rubens in the Wapperstraat. 'Her Majesty,' wrote the chronicler La Serre, 'received great pleasure from her contemplation of the living wonders of his paintings, whose colours Admiration herself must have mixed, since the onlooker never tires of praising their beauty and perfection.'

109   *Isabella-Hélène Rubens*

110   *Hélène Fourment*

In Madrid, by contrast, the Queen Mother's presence in Flemish territory was not welcome, and Philip IV let Isabella know it. Rubens was on his Regent's side. Was not her protection of Marie de Médicis a setback for Richelieu, who, although a Prince of the Church and Spain's ally, spared neither encouragement nor subsidies for the Dutch Protestants who had rebelled against both the Pope and Spain, and was thus a hindrance to the unity of the provinces and a return to peace? The painter had not forgotten the Cardinal's part in preventing the completion of his paintings in honour of Henri IV at the Luxembourg. In art as well as politics the Cardinal was his mortal enemy.

Marie de Médicis had brought with her to Brussels a number of her partisans. These were at first belligerent, but the women of Flanders appear to have tamed them somewhat. They might, however, be made into a source of serious embarrassment for the French. Rubens put his views to Olivarez in a long letter dated 10 August 1631. It is on the scale of a diplomatic report; but its vehemence, resentment and hatred are no longer the feelings of the passionate pacifist. Rubens even expresses a hope that as a result of the troubles which France will soon experience, 'a large number of Frenchmen will perish, and in this way that cruel nation will be weakened.' He adds that 'even if it were necessary to disburse new subsidies, I believe the King's wealth could not be better used for the benefit of our stability and security than in encouraging a civil war in France.'

For the moment the Spaniards tried to provoke it in Holland, sending a flotilla to Zeeland to establish a bridgehead for an invasion of the rebel provinces. The expedition failed, and Rubens had to be sent secretly to the Hague to straighten matters out. This mission, observed the French Ambassador, 'became known, and much displeased certain persons who thus learned in what affairs he was taking part.'

These manœuvres were unworthy of Rubens and he may have realized this. He had always worked in broad daylight, and wearied of his more hidden role. Isabella, who became more and more steeped in piety, was ageing. She was over sixty and saw her end approaching. She suffered much from the knowledge that she had been unable to bring peace to the people whom destiny had placed under her care. The war, which had hardly ceased since the end of the truce between Spain and the United Provinces, had plunged the Netherlands into a situation bordering on catastrophe. Financial ruin, hunger and disorder were everywhere. Antwerp was like an empty carcass beside the abandoned Scheldt. The quays were deserted, the Stock Exchange worked at half-steam, and several shops and industries had closed down. Only the churches were full. Everyone needed God; though perhaps not all of them wished for a purely Spanish one.

112 *Hélène Fourment and her Son, c.* 1635

The Dutch had recovered themselves since Breda, and their fleet was harrying that of Spain. On land they had gained possession of many towns in northern Brabant, and had laid siege to Maestricht, one of the Spaniards' most heavily fortified strongholds in the Netherlands. Extremely disturbed, Isabella sent Rubens at the beginning of August 1632 to Liège, to sound out the intentions of the representatives of the United Provinces. He at once forgot his resolutions and left. He journeyed several times between Liège and Brussels; but on 30 August Maestricht fell. The people were discontented, and the nobility and the army blamed Spain. On 9 September the Regent decided, for the first time for thirty-two years, to convoke the States-General of the Netherlands. They called for the immediate opening of peace negotiations with Holland.

Rubens was of course sent to the Hague as the Infanta's representative to follow the discussions. Unexpectedly, however, the States-General protested in the name of its prerogatives; their real reason was that they saw Rubens as the agent of Spain rather than of the States-General. He had been the servant of Madrid too often not to espouse the Spanish cause, in the end, rather than that of Flanders. So the 'resistance' demanded that the 'collaborator' should stay at home and keep out of their affairs. This was a frightful blow for Rubens, who had served the cause of peace all his life, even if he had not refused titles and honours. He did not, therefore, go to the Hague; but it was as well that he did not: Spain deprived the Infanta of her power to negotiate in the King's name, so that, without a mandate, the deputies talked to no purpose. Naturally the conference failed as a result; and on 1 December 1633 Isabella died.

The country was at the end of its tether, and revolt threatened everywhere. Spain did not give in, however, but sent as the new Governor of the Netherlands the King's own brother, the Cardinal-Infante Don Ferdinand, who was to turn the military situation into one favourable to the South. The war began again in even greater earnest.

Having lost his protectress as well as the goodwill of his country-men, Rubens decided once and for all to renounce politics. He returned to his studio, and announced to Peiresc on 18 December 1634 his final decision to abandon diplomacy. From now on he would concentrate on his painting, his family and his household.

In 1630, the year of his second marriage, he had painted on the orders of the Regent, for the Church of St-Jacques-sur-Coudenberg in Brussels, a large altarpiece which is today in the Kunsthistorisches Museum, Vienna: the *Ildefonso Altarpiece (Pl. 113)*. It is a tumultuous Baroque composition in which the colours positively sing in their diversity, and where the light spreads in a cascade of snow and gold, with trickles of opal, carmine and garnet. It is dazzling like mirrors, and vibrates like an orchestra.

The side-panels contain somewhat flattering portraits of the Arch-duke Albert and Isabella, which share in the general movement of the painting. The sculptural quality of the poses, the voluminousness of the draperies and the broadness of the gestures, evoke the family group Rubens had painted thirty years before of the Gonzagas, in the famous painting in Mantua. On the reverse was a Holy Family in a garden. The panels were sawn through their thickness at the beginning of the eighteenth century to make one picture: *The Holy Family under an Apple Tree*, also in the Kunsthistorisches Museum.

Angelica and the Hermit can be dated between 1630 and 1635, in the period of the numerous portraits and nudes of Hélène. The painting, whose subject is drawn from the *Orlando Furioso* of Ariosto, has a similar freedom in its treatment of figures: the outlines are bathed in light and blurred as if by ecstatic shivers. It is now in the Kunsthis-torisches Museum, and was copied or interpreted by followers of Rubens. Watteau seems to have remembered it in his *Jupiter and Antiope* in the Louvre; and indeed the whole eighteenth century from Boucher to Fragonard seems to be latent in the marvellous body of Angelica, whose rhythms are already those of Renoir's bathers and Matisse's odalisques *(Pl. 114)*.

113 *The Ildefonso Altarpiece*, 1630. Central panel

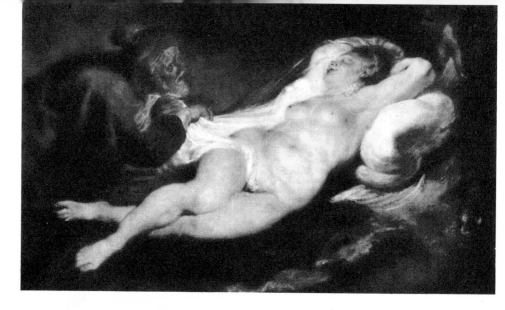

114 *Angelica and the Hermit, c.* 1635

'Body of woman that so tender is...' Once more Rubens, having painted for the Church Virgins, Saints and Martyrs, gave himself up to his triumphant pagan festival of the flesh, impelled equally

115 *Garden of Love,* 1630-35

116   *Diana Bathing*, 1630-35

by his sensuousness and his taste for allegory and legend. In the
same period (1630-35) he painted such important works as *Diana
Bathing* (Boymans-van Beuningen Museum, Rotterdam) *(Pl. 116)*;
Adoration of the Magi (King's College, Cambridge); *Garden of Love*
(Prado) *(Pl. 115)*; and *Virgin and Saints* (Museum of Toledo). The
last work was painted for the Augustinians of Malines, and 'paid
for by alms and by the tanners' guild: 620 fl. 1631.' Finally there
was his decorative scheme for the ceiling of the banqueting hall in
the Palace of Whitehall, London, which Charles I had ordered from

117 *Bathsheba at the Fountain, c.* 1635

118 *The Apotheosis of James I*

him during his diplomatic mission in 1629-30, and in which he was to represent the glorification of Charles's father James I. The scheme, paid for in four instalments totalling £3000 was probably finished in 1634 and placed in position two years later.

To carry out this vast work Rubens divided the huge ceiling into nine sections comprising three large paintings and two smaller ones. The three central panels represented *The Union of England and Scotland*, *The Apotheosis of James I (Pl. 118)* and *The Blessings of the Government of James I*. The other smaller panels illustrated allegories. Before starting work, the painter, as usual, produced sketches, done with a virtuosity which age had not lessened, for approval by Charles I. These are in fact masterpieces. Their grandeur of form and richness of colouring are quite exceptional. Rubens, who set great store by the approval of the King, an enlightened collector and patron of the arts who might well be the source of further commissions, put his best efforts into them. Particular mention must be made of *The Apotheosis of James I*, for the great central composition of the ceiling, in which the departed sovereign is carried up towards eternal glory, surrounded by cherubs holding emblems and accompanied by figures of Religion, Zeal, Honour and Victory (Hermitage, Leningrad).

In *The Union of England and Scotland* the infant Prince of Wales (the future Charles I) supported by allegorical figures representing the two countries, is crowned by Minerva (Boymans-van Beuningen Museum, Rotterdam). The study for the detail from *The Blessings of James I*, representing Peace embracing Abundance, is treated with stupefying brilliance and virtuosity. The speed with which Rubens habitually 'captured' his female figures must be without parallel.

Comparing sketches with the final paintings one notices that, as between the layout and the mural painting, Rubens carried out several transformations, in terms both of the demands of ceiling decoration and of the architectural framework. Having completed this huge scheme in his studio in Antwerp, however, he did not supervise its installation, which took place at the beginning of 1636. 'Having now conceived a horror of courts,' he wrote to Peiresc on 16 March, 'I have sent my painting to England by carrier. It is now installed, and my friends write to me that the king is very pleased.'

The Whitehall ceiling, affected by damp and spoiled by unfortunate restorations, was taken down at the beginning of the Second World War. The process of cleaning revealed everywhere on it the impetuous 'handwriting' of the master's attack on the subject: his great brush-strokes, his verve, his breadth of conception, and above all his lightness and suppleness of touch which transforms the turgid rhetoric of the Baroque into a marvellous feast for the eye.

He found in the decoration of the Banqueting Hall problems parallel to those of the Luxembourg. In Paris he had had to transform inglorious events into brilliant actions, and turn a scheming virago into a peerless queen, wife and mother. In London it was a question of exalting a king who was not merely an oddity but repulsively ugly, weak and timid, and whose reign had been entirely without lustre. The painter got round the difficulty by means of allegory and lyricism. His humanism, nourished by his knowledge of the great Italian mural painters, permeates these evocations, in which rhythms, volumes and colours contribute to the general atmosphere of eloquence and joy. He is like a force of nature. Where others struggled, anxiously and even fearfully, with such enormous tasks, Rubens allowed his Baroque vitality to sweep him away in the intoxication of creation. He seized the task as he seized life itself, and launched himself into it as he had done into politics, or the arms of Hélène; with all the violence and passion and enthusiasm that earns for him the epithet 'superhuman', since men of the stamp of Rubens, Michelangelo, Titian and Delacroix no longer exist.

The *Adoration of the Magi* painted for the high altar of the Church of the Dames Blanches at Louvain, and now at King's College, Cambridge, is another version, as full of freedom as it is of brilliance,

119 *Two Men bathing*

of one of Rubens' most frequently-painted subjects. Considering it in conjunction with *The Virgin and Saints*, one realizes how wide-awake his dynamism remained at this time; how ready he was to express himself in rhythms and masses, in fierce or velvety colours, with all the power and enthusiasm of youth. The female saints of the Toledo canvas repeat, perhaps a little insipidly, the obsessive image of Hélène to be found in the *Garden of Love*.

In Rubens' time this painting was known as *La Conversation à la mode*. It shows a gay company of beautiful, not over-shy young women against the magnificent background of a palace, with fluttering cupids who emphasize its idyllic atmosphere.

The painter's diplomatic activities had ended with serious setbacks, and war continued to batter Flanders, which had lost its sovereign and had dark misgivings about her successor. The sufferings of Antwerp continued; but Rubens, racked with gout and exalted by love, seemed to sing. He celebrated life, youth and love; he put colour everywhere, and with it an enchanting refinement and seductiveness. For there is enormous charm in these tête-à-têtes, these sentimental strolls and whisperings, these balls at which each dancer loves and is happy as if he were alone in the world.

The Baroque impulse becomes calmed now; rhythms grow gentler. On the threshold of old age, a man whose life has been a very full one now writes a page of love, gathering together for it all his favourite themes: landscape, allegory, anecdote, feminine beauty —all in honour of Hélène.

'For the moment,' he wrote to Peiresc[66] on 18 December 1634, 'I am so busy preparing for the arrival of the Cardinal-Infante at the end of this month that I have time neither to write nor to live.' Nevertheless he continued to acquire works of art, as another part of this letter proves; to embellish his house in Antwerp; and to concern himself with many other matters, in particular with the damage to himself caused by a German engraver in Paris in copying his engravings without permission. The German was appealing against his conviction, and Rubens asks Peiresc to commend his 'just cause to the president or to friends of his among the council members.' He adds, 'On the letters your Lordship sends me it would be good to write, instead of "gentleman in ordinary to the household etc.", "secretary to His Catholic Majesty in his secret or privy council."' This was not vanity; but despite what he had said and written the painter had not quite renounced politics. The new Governor's nomination gave a fillip to his hopes.

On 17 April 1635 the Cardinal-Infante Don Ferdinand of Austria, Regent of the Spanish Netherlands, made his 'joyous entry' into Antwerp. The town was given up to rejoicing—in appearance at any rate. In fact it had other things to think about than this ceremonial occasion. All the guilds had been mobilized to decorate the streets and the eleven triumphal arches which had been erected along the route. Fifty thousand florins had been put in the hands of the municipality: 70,000 were spent, and more taxes had to be raised, amid vain protests. Rubens devised and directed the whole scheme of decorations, including the triumphal arches and the 'theatres': vast monumental assemblages of sculpture and pictures in the manner of church altars. He was paid only 5,000 florins for his pains.

Some idea of this vast scheme of ornamentation can be gained from the engravings by Theodor van Thulden which illustrate the commemorative work of Gaspart Gevaert, *Pompa introitus Fernandini*. As usual the painter left nothing to chance. His hand and eye were everywhere, and in spite of a sudden attack of gout he directed the work with complete authority. His team consisted of the best artists in Antwerp: the painters Jacob Jordaens, Theodor Rombouts, Jean de la Barre, Cornelis Schut, Erasmus Quellin, and two sons of Hendrik van Baelen; the sculptors van Mildert, Luc Fay d'Herbe and Van den Eynde; Gevaert supplied the inscriptions.

Rubens' sketches are witness to his gifts as a conceiver of spectacles; they are in the best traditions of both popular art and of the northern Baroque style. The mixture of sculpture, paintings and trompe-

120   *The Meeting of Infante Ferdinand and the King of Hungary in Nördlingen,
c. 1635*

l'œil was well-calculated to excite the popular eye on the day of the 'joyous entry' with its fantasy, rich colouring, and crowded detail, and to blend with the movement of the crowds themselves.

The sketches are entirely by Rubens' hand, as are the two paintings for the 'theatre' erected near the Church of St George. The rest were painted by collaborators and retouched by the artist. The two paintings, in a fairly bad state, represent *The Prince's Journey from Barcelona to Genoa* beneath an allegory of *The Anger of Neptune* (Dresden Gallery), and *The Meeting of Infante Ferdinand and the King of Hungary in Nördlingen* (Prado). They add nothing to the painter's glory *(Pl. 120)*.

More attractive, owing to their inventiveness and rich ornamentation, are the paintings for the 'theatre' erected at the bridge of St Jean representing *Business deserting Antwerp* (Hermitage, Leningrad), and those for both sides of the triumphal arch of Money which belong to the Museum of Antwerp. Other designs for this scheme of decorations are in the Museums of Brussels, Aix-la-Chapelle, Lille and Stockholm, in the Vienna Academy, and at Windsor Castle. It is usual to consider as belonging with them, since Gevaert included it in his *Pompa introitus Fernandini*, the design commissioned from Rubens by the magistrature of Antwerp three years later for a triumphal chariot for the annual town procession *(ommegang)*, and to celebrate Ferdinand's victory over the Dutch at Calloo on 21 June 1638. The painter conceived a magnificent vehicle of lively design, edged with arabesques and crowded with symbolic figures clothed in ample draperies, and with bunches of flags and trophies, on which the victorious Governor rode in triumph. The design of the chariot is in the Museum of Antwerp.

Through his decoration of the streets of Antwerp for the 'joyous entry' of 1635, Rubens' art as a producer and arranger of public spectacles became known to the mass of the people. Until this time he had worked only for princes and the clergy, and the parishes of Antwerp knew only the religious side of his art. But in this way the master of the *Coup de Lance* became one of the few great artists to 'go out into the streets' to participate in a popular scheme for the pleasure of thousands of people. Not until the revolutionary festivities in which David played a part was this to happen again.

Rubens, confined to his bed, was unable to take part in the ceremony for the Cardinal-Infante; but Ferdinand, knowing of Rubens' services to the King of Spain, called on him. The gesture flattered the people of Antwerp, though some of them wondered if their compatriot had not now become more Spanish than Flemish.

A few weeks later, Rubens acquired the superb mansion of Steen, at Elewijt, a few kilometres from Brussels. This impressive dwelling, which still has its ancient air in spite of alterations and reconstructions, was at that time surrounded by fields and woods crossed by a water-course. Rubens painted numerous landscapes there, and these show what the house and its surroundings were like when he moved there with his family. He acquired at the same time the title of 'Seigneur du Steen' which was to figure at the head of his tombstone.

Since 1627 Rubens had owned a property to the north of Antwerp called the 'Hof van Orsele', where he often went for a rest. There was a picturesque house there, on an islet in the middle of a small lake. But Steen is very different: it is a feudal manor guarded with turrets and possessing a keep—a very suitable dwelling for the court painter and secretary to the Privy Council of the King of Spain, the Ambassador dubbed knight by both Philip IV and Charles I, whose social position was almost as princely as his fortune. He was now a landed proprietor too.

His choice of the countryside near Brussels may have been motivated by a desire to avoid offending his fellow-citizens of Antwerp in this extremely difficult period of their country's history. He may also have wanted to be nearer to the court. But Rubens was more concerned with the demands of his position than with mere show; and in any case his family was still growing. In May 1635, the month in which he bought Steen, Hélène had given birth to their third child, Isabella-Hélène. Eleven months later Rubens was appointed Court Painter to the Cardinal-Infante.

This belligerent person had decided to avenge Richelieu's signing of the agreement with the Dutch by taking possession of Trier, then under French protection. At once Louis XIII declared war on Spain and invaded Luxembourg. His troops, having joined those of the *stathouder*, invaded Brabant. Ferdinand counter-attacked with 15,000 Imperial troops and pushed the enemy back.

For the first time war had reached the territory of the United Provinces, and the States-General were alarmed. Was this the long-awaited chance to conclude a peace treaty? Rubens must have danced with satisfaction at Steen. And now Bishop Antoine Triest brought forward plans for talks and negotiations. The painter already saw himself as His Catholic Majesty's emissary; he suggested going to Holland with his two sons on the pretext of looking at works of art. It was not a good time for such a journey but Rubens thought little of it and hurried to Brussels to offer his services to Ferdinand.

The Cardinal-Infante was not inclined, as Isabella had been, to listen to and follow his advice kindly. He admired the painter, but he had no need of more diplomats. Besides this, the French Ambassador skilfully contrived things so that Rubens failed to receive his passport. The Holland journey did not take place. Rubens returned to Steen, where he drew all the folds of his dignity about him to write to Peiresc[67] that in case there had been any talk, the fact was that he 'had not been given elbow-room,' and that faced with the difficulty of obtaining a passport, he had 'at once contrived to waste time on purpose' and had 'sought every means of avoiding involvement.' He adds hypocritically: 'Since, besides this, there was no lack of people anxious to obtain such a mission, I have been able to save my peace of mind, and, thank God, here I am quietly at home.' But he would have given up his 'peace of mind' like a shot.

Despite more and more frequent and severe crises, Rubens painted in 1635 and 1636 three of his most marvellous works: the great sketch of *The Miracles of St Benedict (Pl. 122)*; *The Carrying of the Cross (Pl. 121)*; and *The Martyrdom of St Livinus (Pl. 123)*. In addition he began at the end of 1636 the decorations for the Torre de la Parada, near Madrid. At fifty-nine he was still in possession of his powers; indeed he seemed never to have had such creative strength.

The Miracles of St Benedict is a sketch for a painting which was never executed, probably for a Benedictine Abbey. It now belongs to the Royal Museums of Belgium. It illustrates an episode from the Golden Legend which tells how Totila, the king of the Goths, in order to test the shrewdness of St Benedict, sent him in place of himself one of his squires sumptuously attired; and how the pious

monk recognized the fraud and confounded the false king. This scene is accompanied by an evocation of the healing of St Benedict of the sick who are massed below the cloisters of Monte Cassino imploring the saint with pathetic gestures, while Totila himself, dismounted, prepares to go and render homage to him.

This superimposition of several different subjects is Rubens' opportunity to demonstrate his knowledge and ingenuity. The composition is marked off by oblique movements which tend to unbalance it, but its equilibrium is restored by the distribution of

122   *The Miracles of St Benedict*

the masses. It is at once full of density and full of dynamism, and its vitality of expression is extraordinary. Delacroix's admiration for the picture was such that in 1841 he made a copy of it which, exhibited next to the original in the Royal Museums, Brussels, is particularly instructive about the great Romantic painter's understanding and assimilation of Rubens' style.

The sketch may possibly have been for a painting for the abbey of Afflighem, for which Rubens painted, almost in the same period, the pathetic *Carrying of the Cross*. Rubens kept it in his studio, and it was given by his heirs to the painter Gaspar de Crayer in gratitude for his mediation in the sale of twenty-nine of Rubens' works to the King of Spain after the painter's death. In fact, Crayer, who was one of Rubens' warmest admirers, did a great deal of work for Afflighem, a circumstance which is the basis of Max Rooses' contention[68] that *The Miracles of St Benedict* was sold by its owner to the abbey and exhibited there. J. F. M. Michel[69] is of the opinion that the work was intended for the abbey, and that the monks, unable to obtain the finished painting, contented themselves with the sketch, which was found, according to him, in the foreign quarter. After a number of adventures it was acquired in 1881 by King Leopold II of Belgium, and entered the Royal Museums in 1914.

The Carrying of the Cross, commissioned in 1634 by the Abbot of Afflighem for his church's high altar, was painted two years later, and placed in position on 8 April 1637. A manuscript chronicle of the abbey, written in the seventeenth century, and belonging to the Bibliothèque Royale, Brussels, tells us that Rubens, having painted a preliminary sketch, went to Afflighem and amended the composition *(suscepit tabulam a se meliori forma delineandam)* after a visit to the abbey, when he had seen the monumental altar which had been built to receive his work. This first sketch is probably the one which belongs to the Rijksmuseum, Amsterdam. The second, whose dimensions correspond more closely to those of the altar, is in the State Museum, Copenhagen. It is painted in a few strokes,

123   *The Martyrdom of St Livinus*

brown on brown, with white and red highlights. The evolution which has taken place between the two sketches, is noticeable. The concentrated composition of the first becomes stretched out in the second by an upward movement corresponding to the increased height required. Rubens made other sketches on the theme of the ascent of Calvary, which seem previous to the one in the Rijksmuseum. The explanation is that although ignorant as to the shape and size of the surface which would be available, the painter produced, in the heat of the moment—as he did whenever a new subject was suggested to him—numbers of studies in search of a composition and movement. These are particularly revealing about his ideas on the 'preparation' of his paintings *(Pl. 121)*.

The final composition of *The Carrying of the Cross* is one of the grandest and most full of movement that Rubens ever conceived. 'At this date,' writes Fromentin, 'Rubens had painted most of his great works. He was no longer young: he knew everything, and would only have gone on painting, had not death protected his talent from decay. Here there is movement and tumult and agitation: in the figures, gestures, faces, groupings; and in the oblique thrust, diagonal and symmetrical, from bottom right to top left...' Here, there is the most sublime spectacle which the great lyricist of Antwerp ever conceived in his daring or his faith. From this painful climb of Jesus under the weight of the Cross and the whips of the soldiers and the cries of the crowd, broken, brutalized and streaming with blood, towards his death, Rubens creates, by the sheer organization of his warm tones in the resplendent golden light, a glorious progress. The supreme skill lies in this: there is the drama, deeply disturbing; the prostration of Christ; the irritability of the executioners; the pleas of the Holy Women; the panic of the thieves pushed along by the soldiers; tragedy is everywhere. Yet everywhere there is singing; and everything shines with the divine light which announces the presence of the Father. Victory is at hand: the victory of the Son of Man over sin and death.

To express the upward movement of the procession Rubens has multiplied the diagonals and obliquities, and these converge towards the group of horsemen brandishing lances and oriflammes at the summit of the composition. The colouring is admirable, and the handling, rapid and decisive, appears to follow the impulses of the painter's imagination as they occur. The brushwork is bold and flowing, and relieved by more definite strokes. Each element is drawn into a sort of collective excitement which escalates, and forces the onlooker to appreciate the artist's rendering of emotion.

The Martyrdom of St Livinus shares the same mastery. Also in the Royal Museums, this painting was executed for the high altar of the Jesuit church in Ghent. The barbaric horror of the scene, which shows the evangelist of Gaul having his tongue torn out by ruffians and thrown to the dogs, is much lessened by the freshness —not to say, like Fromentin, the gaiety—of the colouring; and by a kind of bound or projection of the whole painting forwards. True to his method, Rubens has once again transformed a discouraging subject into a 'feast for the eye'.

This result would not have been achieved by a work closely conforming to the apologetic and moralizing spirit of the Counter-Reformation; but Rubens, while remaining firmly in control of his means, abandons himself to the Baroque, and fears neither the excessive gesture nor the accumulation of detail. His powerful plastic language, which could not be matched by other painters because it was so much a part of his own exaggerated personality, had considerable influence on Flemish sculptors. One can almost say that they 'sculpted Rubenses,' moderating, like him, the southern exuberance of Bernini through the logical harmonizing of forms and the control of the mind. But while the painter of the *Coup de Lance* gave a powerful internal life to his paintings, that of the work of such men as Erasmus Quellin, André de Nole, Van Mildert or François du Quesnoy, who left Flanders for Rome in 1618 and never returned, remains completely external.

In the general harmony of *The Martyrdom of St Livinus* with its silvery tones, the ochres and browns, the grey-white of the horse rearing against the azured grey of the sky, the gold of the saint's chasuble and his white stole, the pink flesh of the cherubs, the blacks and dark greys of the bandits' armour and clothes, the muscular limbs with their vermilion reflections, the dogs flecked with black and white—all these constitute a sort of dialogue of clearly distinguished tones; while in the centre of the picture flames the vermilion cap of one of the ruffians. The masses jostle together in a controlled confusion, out of which shine the knife streaming with blood held between the teeth of a hideous barbarian, the liturgical ornaments, a shield, and the luminous splashes of hands and shoulders. Above the central group, however, which is dominated by the rearing horse, the composition becomes lighter and more spacious. Two delightful 'putti' precede the avenging angels about to fall on the criminals, and the brutal scene is transformed into a triumphal allegory. This kind of dialogue between heaven and earth is often met with in Rubens' paintings.

It is impossible to imagine that either *The Martyrdom of St Livinus* or *The Carrying of the Cross* might not have been painted entirely by Rubens' hand. His handwriting is everywhere visible. Max Rooses' statement[70] that the middle ground and lower portion of *The Martyrdom of St Livinus* were painted by a collaborator, probably Theodor van Thulden, and retouched by Rubens, is simply staggering.

The sketch, which is noticeably different from the painting in Brussels, is one of the most superbly 'captured' of them all (Boymans-van Beuningen Museum, Rotterdam). Its general rhythm is hardly diminished in the final painting; from small scale to full size (the canvas is over 4.47 metres high) the same lyricism persists, and the same excitement adapts itself to new dimensions, only requiring more expressive forms in the painting and less striking colours in the sketch (in which the cap in the centre is dark red, whereas in the painting it is a fine clear vermilion) *(Pl. 123)*.

124 *Rape of Europa*

In the directness of his expression of life, which is animated by his thought, Rubens excelled all other painters of his time. On the great stage of the Counter-Reformation he set in motion, as no man had done since Michelangelo, men, gods, saints, geniuses and allegories, whose life-blood transfused his brush. He was less concerned with beauty and truth than with life, and in particular with the Christian life in which faith must be strengthened despite the Reformation, and whose goal and end was the glory of God. He stood for the 'new spirit' of the Catholic Church, and against the forces of 'disorder', and his art is as much a monument to his outlook as to his genius.

CHAPTER TEN

Twilight of a god

In the autumn of 1636 Rubens was commissioned to decorate the Torre de la Parada, one of Philip IV's hunting lodges not far from Madrid. On 20 November the Cardinal-Infante Ferdinand wrote to his brother: 'Concerning the paintings Your Majesty orders me to have carried out for the Tower, Rubens has received the commission and tells me that he has already begun work on some of them.' As soon as the decision was made, Rubens had, as usual, seized his brushes and started work. On 30 January 1637 the Governor writes that the frost has not quenched the painter's enthusiasm. 'At the same time,' he adds, 'I fear greatly that the task may be dragging, for Rubens can give no precise answer, but promises only that he and the other painters will not lose an hour of the time.' Rubens was once more in the grip of violent attacks of rheumatism. It was not until a year later, on 21 January 1638, that Ferdinand could announce to the King that the scheme was completed. The paintings were sent to Madrid on 11 March.

The building of the Torre de la Parada included twenty-five rooms for which Rubens had been commanded to paint mythological pictures, hunting scenes and illustrations drawn from Ovid's *Metamorphoses*. Although he was expected to produce all the sketches, the paintings—112 in all—might be by artists of his choice. That is why very few are by his own hand. On those which have been preserved one finds the signatures of Jordaens, Cornelis de Vos, Erasmus Quellin, Theodor van Thulden, Cornelis Schut, Pieter Symons, Thomas Villeboirts, Jacques-Pierre Gouwi and others. All of them observed the style and spirit of the master.

125   *Return from the Fields, c.* 1636

The panels painted by Rubens himself suffered the fate of the whole collection, which was destroyed or dispersed after the sack of the Torre de la Parada in 1710. Some are now in the Prado. They are markedly inferior to the sketches, which are painted with undiminished dexterity, and in whose very free rapid rhythms and airy lightness one can almost observe the movements of the hand. The colouring, enlivened by sudden touches, greens, carmines and yellows, on backgrounds of ochre, is full of warmth. Rubens has perfected the art of launching into space, and there combining figures which dance or fly in daring and fantastic rhythms. He seems to do this almost carelessly, without worrying about the total effect; but his mastery is such that he can afford any caprice; and this he proves in *Aurora and Cephalus, The Fall of Phaeton, Cupid on a Dolphin, The Triumph of the Milky Way,* and *The Fall of Icarus.*

These sketches were given by Charles II to the Duke of Benavente. Some of them are now in collections of aristocratic Spanish families; others are in the Prado, the Royal Museums of Brussels, and various other museums and collections *(Pl. 126)*.

Rubens' attacks of gout were now becoming more and more frequent, and were causing him long weeks of inactivity. He appeared at court less and less often, preferring to stay at Steen among his family and enjoy from his invalid's chair, or from the saddle when his health permitted, the charming landscape which surrounded him.

He had always loved nature and never stopped painting it. In Italy he had wrought the stormy, seismically shaken *Landscape with the Shipwreck of Aeneas;* later there had been *The Farm at Laeken, The Summer* and *The Winter* in the British Royal Collections, and

126 *Mercury and Argus, c.* 1635

127 *Landscape with a Cart at Sundown, c.* 1625-38

many other landscapes inspired by the country round Ekeren, where he had a house—notably the very fine *Return from the Fields* in the Pitti Palace *(Pl. 125)*; the bucolic *Landscape with a Cart at Sundown* (Boymans-van Beuningen Museum) *(Pl. 127)*, which Oldenbourg dates at 1620-25, whereas Prof. Hannema places it after 1630, and Mr Charles Sterling between 1635 and 1638; *Landscape with Shepherds* (National Gallery); *Landscape with Goatherd* in the Pennsylvania Museum, Philadelphia; and others. His time spent at Steen was to Rubens like being in the midst of a fairy-tale, of which he, as a townsman and courtier, had seen only rare episodes. There are hardly any descriptions of landscapes in his letters.

His *Landscape with a Rainbow* in the Museum of Valenciennes *(Pl. 128)*, *The Park of Steen*, of which there is one version in the Kunsthistorisches Museum and another somewhat different in the Dulière Collection, Brussels, and *The Château de Steen in Autumn* (National Gallery) *(Pl. 130)* all belong to 1635 to 1637. They are powerful syntheses of nature, in which the earth seems to live and breathe like a human body. As in his large figure-paintings, Rubens conceives the whole as a kind of spectacle which he brushes in with

128   *Landscape with a Rainbow, c. 1635*

great sweeps, spreading large areas of light among fields and valleys. A turbulent sky dominates, and here the painter allows his vision full rein. Here again is the heroic conception which animates him: a breath of epic which leads the onlooker far away from the traditional Flemish landscape—though he contributed to that too, through his influence on such painters as Jan Wildens and Lucas van Uden.

Rubens had neither the tragic spirituality of Rembrandt nor the constructive logic of Poussin. He was the pure lyricist, the seer whose gaze comprehends the vast movements of the earth, who was always searching for pictorial effects which he embellished with

129   *Hercules and Minerva fighting Mars*

130   *The Château de Steen in Autumn, c. 1636*

the jewels of his palette. He handles to admiration the deep and pale greens, the browns, ochres, whites, carmines and golds, which he also—in, for example, *Landscape with Atalanta*—knows how to orchestrate into a symphony. The romantic elements in *The Park of Steen*, which inspired Watteau and Manet, are in harmony with his breadth of inspiration and with his method of composition, in which the rhythms generously fill the space. The rustic poetry of the *Landscape with Fowler* in the Louvre has a subtle charm; in it the mist and sunshine as in Impressionist painting, are real 'subjects'. Even before Claude, Rubens had dared to look at the sun itself and paint it.

His health continued to worsen. On 8 April 1637 Balthazar Moretus wrote to his friend Frans van Raphelengien of Leyden that the painter was now suffering so much that he could not sketch even the smallest subjects, and had not managed to provide any work for the engraver. Some months later Philip Chifflet wrote

131 *Study of Trees*

to Cardinal di Bagno, former Papal Nuncio in Brussels: 'Rubens has
not yet recovered from a long and painful illness, which reduced
him to extremity. He is at present convalescent.' On 15 February 1539
Rubens wrote to Chifflet[71] about an order of the Cardinal's for some
tapestry cartoons: 'I beg of you that you will represent to His Excel-

lency that the troubles I suffer in my person, which often take the form of gout, not permitting me to manage pen or brush, and taking as their usual seat my right hand, prevent me above all from making drawings on a small scale.'

132 *Landscape*

Once again Rubens looked at himself *(Pls. 136, 137).* As he had done in *Tribute to Justus Lipsius,* in his self-portrait with Isabella Brandt, and in the *Portrait of Rubens with a Hat,* now in Florence, where he appears in the fullness of his maturity. But today it was another matter: he was old, tired and ill. His look was weary and a little distant; the avid observer of life had now retired from affairs, and lived alone with his family, in the company of nature, to continue the dialogue he had begun with gods and heroes, saints and his

257

133   *La Kermesse, c.* 1635

Creator himself, with the fields, the trees and the changing light of his land at Steen. He who had formerly opposed to each other the giants of Olympus or of history, who had confronted his own stormy soul with the drama of Golgotha, now considered only the

relative strength of green and ochre on his ploughed land, the fall of the light on the trees, and the gold of the sunsets.

His self-portrait in the Kunsthistorisches Museum, for which there is a preparatory drawing in the Louvre, is that of a worn old

134   *A Shepherd and Mercury*

man. The eyelids are heavy, the eyes dull, the cheeks flabby. The artist, whose hand is on his sword-hilt, is dressed in black and wears a wide-brimmed hat. His wife was at this time twenty-five years old.

As sometimes happens when age and illness turn a man's thoughts towards death, Rubens turned towards his country, his childhood and his family. He painted, in celebration of Flanders, the bacchanal in the spirit of Brueghel the Elder and of Teniers which is known as *La Kermesse* and hangs in the Louvre. It was finished, according to the tradition, in a single day, and is dated about 1635-36 *(Pl. 133)*.

It contains all the traditional elements of Flemish life: the tavern, the tables in the open air, casks being emptied, pitchers, cooking-pots

135   *Apollo, Diana and the Niobids*

136 *Self-Portrait, c.* 1638-40

137 *Self-Portrait*. Drawing for the painting (pl. 136)

and jugs; the piper, and the couples intertwined, drinking, laughing,
embracing, dancing, rolling on the ground to kiss and hug, hands
fumbling at necklines and under skirts. It is an extraordinarily wild
ritual of the senses, and it moves in curves like those of a snake
across the grass. In the space gorged with light and bathed in azure
the air moves freely: warm and lively colours, tinted with rose, lilac,
green and orange, emphasize the turning movement which appears
against the warm golden-brown background, like a series of multi-

138 *The Judgment of Paris, c. 1635*

coloured discs, reminiscent of the 'simultanéisme' of Delaunay.
The figures, seen in full flight, are 'captured' with an alert brush,
in swift, light touches. The speed expresses the vitality of the forces
released; and often a single brushstroke defines pose, form, mass,
light and movement at one and the same time. Rubens had never
before achieved the delirious power which electrifies this truculent
Flemish crowd in full and flagrant orgy.

The concentration and crowding of the figures in their noisy gaiety
contrasts with the almost bare landscape in which *La Kermesse* is set;
but the more the swirl of dancers becomes separated from the central
group, the fewer in number these are seen to be, and the less definite
the dancing couples become—as if they were melting into light

and space. This suggestion of time, which little by little absorbs the movement and force of life, was something new in Flemish art. Many painters were to take up the idea—in a different form, admittedly—but expressing the same attitude.

As if to hold on to life and, perhaps, Hélène too, Rubens painted more beautiful women: *The Offering to Venus*, now in Vienna; and *The Rape of the Sabines (Pl. 140)*, *Village Dances* and *Nymphs and Satyrs (Pl. 141)*, now in the Prado. Like *The Three Graces* and *The Judgment of Paris (Pl. 138)*, they display the Fleming's paganism and love of the flesh without equivocation. All these canvases were painted between 1638 and 1640. There is still freedom and life in the embraces and dancing of *The Offering to Venus*. Inspired by a Titian in the Prado which Rubens had copied, the painting weaves a pattern in which nymphs and satyrs, ladies and gallants mingle amidst a crowd of boisterous cherubs.

139   *The Judgment of Paris, c. 1638*

At the beginning of 1638 Rubens sent to Florence, for the Medicis, at the request of the painter Sustermans who was engaged in enlarging their gallery, a canvas entitled *The Evils of War*, which is now in the Pitti Palace. Rubens, writing to his friend on 12 March, describes this picture with a minuteness of detail which is all the more necessary since the work is a rather obscurely symbolical one. He adds in a postscript that if the long journey in its packing case has affected its colours Sustermans is authorized to repair them 'wherever an accident or my own carelessness has made this necessary.'

This was the first time he had admitted to any weakening of his hand. It was also the first time he had ever invited a colleague to retouch his work unsupervised. It was a clear-sighted admission: *The Evils of War* does in fact betray a definite lessening of his powers:

140   *The Rape of the Sabines, c.* 1638-40

141　*Nymphs and Satyrs, c.* 1638-40

it is careless as to form and uneven in its surface treatment, and its
colours are dissonant.

The Martyrdom of St Peter, however, which was painted at the
same period, has great vigour. Probably Rubens' strength waxed
and waned as his attacks receded and advanced. This painting, for
the Church of St Peter in Cologne, contains much broad relief. Its
conception is dexterous but qualified by a certain heaviness. The
colouring has the warmth common to the most important paintings
of this period.

In 1639 he painted for the Convent of St Thomas of Mala Strana
in Prague *The Miracle of St Augustine* and *The Martyrdom of St Thomas*,
which contain real achievements, both in the richness of the colouring,
particularly that of the vestments of St Augustine, and in the pathos

142 *Child playing the Violin*

143   *The Three Graces, c.* 1639

of St Thomas' expression. The last canvases on which Rubens worked
—*The Rape of the Sabines, The Sabine Peace, Perseus and Andromeda*,
and a *Hercules* were commissioned by Philip IV of Spain. His
brother Ferdinand mentions them frequently in his letters to him
and says that their execution is suffering much from the painter's
ill-health. The *Hercules* is lost; *Perseus and Andromeda* was finished
by Jordaens, and *The Rape of the Sabines* by another artist. *The
Sabine Peace*, which was also known as *The Reconciliation of the*

144 *Rape of Hippodamia, c.* 1635

Romans and Sabines, was destroyed in the fire at the Royal Palace of Madrid in 1734.

On 16 September 1639 Rubens, back in Antwerp after a long stay at Steen, decided to visit his notary in order to make arrangements for his will. His illness was gaining ground. By February 1640 the painter had lost the use of his hands, which were paralysed with rheumatism. In spite of the efforts of the court physicians sent by Ferdinand, the paralysis was steadily approaching his heart. On 27 May he had a new will drawn up. Three days later, at noon on 30 May, he died. Nine months later Hélène gave birth to a daughter, thus bearing witness, as some people say, to the painter's vitality, despite his illness.

Gerbier wrote: 'M. Rubens died three days ago, so that now Jordaens is the first painter here.'

On the day of his death, his body was taken to the family vault of the Fourments in the Church of St James: it was here that the funeral service took place on 2 June. In 1642 his widow, who three years later was to marry an ex-magistrate of Antwerp, caused to be placed above his tombstone, in a rich marble setting, a painting by the dead man which is said to be also a family portrait: *The Madonna and Child surrounded by Saints*. It is a thoroughly thought-out composition of his maturity, and is both warmly and skilfully painted. In it the face of St George is perhaps that of Rubens himself. If it is true

145   *Triumph of Venus*

146 *Women and Children round the Hearth*

that Mary Magdalene, who is naked to the waist and whose attractions are very generously displayed, represents Hélène Fourment, her action in placing the painting in her husband's mortuary chapel was a somewhat ambiguous one. The epitaph on the ledger-stone was composed in 1755 by Canon van Parys, the painter's great-nephew.

The first sale of paintings from Rubens' studio produced about 52,000 florins; a subsequent sale produced another 8,000. The King of Spain acquired one lot of canvases for 27,100 florins. Gerbier took part in the bidding on behalf of the King of England, and there were also collectors at the sales from Germany, France, Britain and elsewhere. Some of the works were bought by the Fourment family.

Several painters, friends or collaborators of the dead man's, who had helped with the inventory or the sale, each received, in accordance with his will, one of their master's works. In the same way certain physicians, an innkeeper, and various shopkeepers were compensated for their trouble.

In June 1959 the *Adoration of the Magi*, painted in 1634 for the Dames Blanches of Louvain, which had become the property of the Duke of Westminster, was put up for sale in London. It is now at King's College, Cambridge. The price paid, 3,770,000 francs (£270,000), was the highest ever paid for a painting.

Text References

[1] Jan-Baptist died in 1600 (childless)

[2] In 1590 married Simon du Parcq, who died in 1606

[3] Died in 1580

[4] Died in 1583

[5] Died in 1611. He was married to Maria de Moy, in Antwerp, and they had two children, Claire and Philip, the latter born shortly after his father's death

[6] Paul Jamot, *Rubens*. Paris 1935

[7] Leo van Puyvelde, *La Peinture flamande au siècle de Bosch et de Brueghel*. Brussels 1962

[8] Isaac Bullart, *Académie des Sciences et des Arts, contenant les Vies et les Éloges Historiques des Hommes Illustres qui ont excellé en ces professions depuis environ quatre siècles parmi diverses Nations de l'Europe*. Paris-Brussels-Amsterdam 1682

[9] Roger de Piles, *Abrégé de la vie des Peintres, avec des Réflexions sur leurs ouvrages et un Traité du peintre parfait, de la connaissance des dessins et de l'utilité des estampes*. Paris 1699

[10] Rudolf Oldenbourg, 'Abhandlungen über Rubens', *Münchener Jahrbuch der Bildenden Kunst*, Vol XI, 1919. W. Bode, *Peter Paul Rubens*. Berlin 1922. Christopher Norris, 'Rubens before Italy', *The Burlington Magazine*, Vol LXXVI, 1940

[11] A. de Hevesy, 'Rubens et la Franche-Comté', *Gazette des Beaux-Arts*

[12] Leo van Puyvelde, 'A Self-portrait by the young Rubens', *Gazette des Beaux-Arts*, Vol LVI, 1944

[13] In 1604-5 when this portrait was painted Vincenzo II was about ten years old and Francesco eighteen or nineteen. The model is a young man and not a child

[14] Leo van Puyvelde, *Rubens*. op. cit.

[15] F.M. Haberditzl in *Kunstgeschichtliche Anzeigen* 1909. id. in *Jahrbuch der Kunsthistorischen Sammlungen des allerhöchsten Kaiserhauses in Wien*, Vol XXX, 1912

[16] Rubens to Annibale Chieppio. Valladolid, 24 May 1603. Gonzaga Archives, Mantua

[17] Rubens to Chieppio. Valladolid, 17 July 1603. Gonzaga Archives, Mantua

[18] Rubens to Chieppio. Valladolid, 24 May 1603. Gonzaga Archives, Mantua

[19] Dr Gustav Glück, *Rubens, Van Dyck und ihr Kreis*. Vienna 1933

[20] In 1869 the *Baptism of Christ* belonged, after many changes of owners, to Baron de Laage of Lille; he offered the painting to the Brussels Museum, but it was refused. The next owner, Joseph de Bom, bequeathed it to the Antwerp Museum, where it has been since 1869

[21, 22] Rubens to Chieppio. Rome, 29 July 1606. Gonzaga Archives, Mantua

[23] Rubens to Chieppio. Rome, 28 April 1607. Archives, Antwerp

24 Rubens to Chieppio. Rome, 2 December 1606. Gonzaga Archives, Mantua
25 Rubens to Chieppio. Rome, 2 February 1608. Gonzaga Archives, Mantua
26 Roberto Longhi, *Vita Artistica* 1927. Ludwig Burchard in *Pinacoteca*, I, 1928-9
27, 28 Rubens to Chieppio. Rome, 2 February 1608. Gonzaga Archives, Mantua
29 Rubens to Chieppio. Rome, 23 February 1608. Gonzaga Archives, Mantua
30 Rubens to Chieppio. Rome, 28 October 1609. Gonzaga Archives, Mantua
31 Charles Ruelens and Max Rooses, *La Correspondance et documents épistolaires de P.P. Rubens.* 6 vols. Antwerp 1887-1909. Paul Colin, Paris 1926, has published a limited selection of extracts, freely translated
32 Rubens to Jacques de Bie. Antwerp, 11 May 1611. Royal Archives, Brussels
33, 34 Roger de Piles, *Dissertation sur les ouvrages des plus fameux peintres,* dedicated to the Duc de Richelieu, 1681
35 Palazzo Pitti, Florence. Rubens, his brother Philip, Justus Lipsius and Jan Wouver. Rubens used a portrait painted by Abraham Janssens, engraved by Pieter de Jode, for the features of Justus Lipsius who died in 1606
36 Rubens to Johann Faber. Antwerp, December 1610. Archives of the Foundling Hospital, Rome
37 Rubens to Sir Dudley Carleton. Antwerp, 28 April 1618. Public Record Office, London
38 Charles Sterling, 'Manet et Rubens', *L'Amour de l'Art,* No. 8, 1932
39 So-called after its description in the catalogue of Jeremias Wildens († 1653), who owned the picture. *Cauvenus,* is a contraction of *koude Venus,* the 'cold Venus'. Another view is that this work illustrates the proverb: Sine Baccho et Cerere frigat Venus (Hunger and Thirst make Love turn cold).
40 Hildebrand, *Études franciscaines,* XLV, 1935
41 Respectively: Chester Dale Collection, National Gallery, Washington, Stettenheim Trust New York and Dulière Collection, Brussels. *The Ethiopian King (Balthazar)* belonged during the last War to Marshal Göring
42 Rubens to Archduke Albert. Antwerp, 18 March 1614. Royal Archives, Brussels
43 Rubens to Sir Dudley Carleton. Antwerp, 28 April 1618. Public Record Office, London
44 Rubens to Carleton. Antwerp, 12 May 1618. Public Record Office, London
45 A slightly different version belongs to the Berlin Museum, and there are two others in the National Gallery and the Hermitage Museum, Leningrad
46 Eugène Fromentin, *Les Maîtres d'autrefois. Belgique, Hollande.* Paris 1876
47 An unknown writer to the Earl of Arundel. Antwerp, 17 July 1620. Collection Duke of Norfolk
48 Rubens to Carleton. Antwerp, 26 May 1618. Public Record Office, London
49, 50 Rubens to Peiresc. Paris, 13 May 1625. The Royal Library, The Hague
51 Rubens to William Trumbull. Antwerp, 13 September 1621. Public Record Office, London
52 Sir Birkey Smith, *Dr Otto Sperling's Selvbiografi oversat i Undrag after Originalhandskriftet.* Copenhagen 1885. Translated in *Repertorium für Kunstwissenschaft,* X, 1887
53 Roger de Piles, *Abrégé de la Vie de Rubens* in *Conversations sur la connaissance de la peinture et sur le Jugement qu'on doit faire des tableaux.* Paris 1677, then printed separately

[54] Rubens to Peiresc. Paris, 13 May 1625. The Royal Library, The Hague
[55] The Royal Library, The Hague. Gerard Foundation
[56] Rubens to Pieter Peck. Antwerp, 30 Septembre 1623. Royal Archives, Brussels
[57] Rubens to Jan Brandt. Antwerp, 20 July 1625. Herzögliche Bibliothek, Wolfenbuttel
[58] Rubens to Jan Brandt. Brussels, 25 August 1625. Herzögliche Bibliothek, Wolfenbuttel
[59] Rubens to Pierre Dupuy. Antwerp, 27 January 1628. Bibliothèque Nationale, Paris
[60] Max Rooses, *L'Œuvre de Rubens*, 5 vols. Antwerp 1886-92
[61] Rubens to Pierre Dupuy. Antwerp, 15 July 1626. Museo Civico, Turin
[62] Exhibited in the Plantin-Moretus Museum, Antwerp
[63] Ludwig Burchard and R.A. d'Hulst, *Catalogue Tekeningen van P.P. Rubens*. Antwerp 1956
[64] Francisco Pacheco, *El Arte de la Pintura*. Madrid 1648
[65] Rubens to Pierre Dupuy. Antwerp, October 1630. Bibliothèque Nationale, Paris
[66] Rubens to Peiresc. Antwerp, 18 December 1634. Bibliothèque Nationale, Paris
[67] Rubens to Peiresc. Antwerp, 16 March 1636. Original lost, copy in the Bibliothèque Méjanes, Aix-en-Provence
[68] Max Rooses, *L'Œuvre de Rubens*. op. cit.
[69] J.F.M. Michel, *Histoire de la Vie de P.P. Rubens*. Brussels 1771
[70] Max Rooses, *L'Œuvre de Rubens*. op. cit.
[71] Rubens to Philip Chifflet. Antwerp, 15 February 1639. Bagno Archives, Mantua

List of Illustrations

Page numbers in bold type indicate colour plates

Index

(References are to the text only; the plates are listed on pp. 277-81.)